Praise for
The Five O'Clock Club and *Through the Brick Wall*

"On behalf of eight million New Yorkers, I commend and thank The Five O'Clock Club. Keep the faith and keep America working!"
> David N. Dinkins, Mayor,
> The City of New York

"Kate Wendleton has written a sage and sensible book for the turbulent 90's. She believes you need to take a proactive approach to getting the kind of job you want, and she shows you how to get it in *Through the Brick Wall!*"
> Harvey Mackay
> author of *Swim with the Sharks Without Being Eaten Alive* and *Sharkproof*

"Everyone who has met Kate knows that she has a genius for caring about others. Her inspiring energy and wide practical knowledge about job hunting are packed into this wonderful book. It will be of great help to all who read it."
> David Rottman, vice president and manager,
> Career Services, Chemical Bank, New York City

"Everyone talks about 'taking charge' of their lives; Kate Wendleton shows you how. One of the savviest and most effective career counselors that I know teaches that—even in the toughest of times—you can (and deserve to) find work that is right for you."
> Robert Mintz, director of Human Resources,
> Time, Inc., Magazines

"In eighteen years of career counseling and coaching, I have seen nothing as good as this book. It combines sound, practical advice about the hiring process with profound wisdom and humor regarding the inner issues stirred up by transition. Today's job market is the toughest I've seen, and it requires the combination Kate has struck: shrewdness about the hiring process and the courage to face inner issues. Great work!"
> William Pilder, chairman, TransKey

"Kate Wendleton offers a wealth of pragmatic, uplifting advice for the job seeker. A person who follows Kate's formula would certainly get my attention, even if I'd already rejected his or her résumé."
> Carole F. St. Mark, president,
> Pitney Bowes Logistics Systems
> & Business Services

"*Through the Brick Wall* is a great book for a success-oriented transitional executive. It breaks the process into do-able steps that are easy to understand."
> Albert Prendergast, senior vice president,
> Human Resources, Mastercard International

"I am living proof that you can change your career for the better with the techniques described in *Through the Brick Wall*. Take a look at Chapter 2."
> Bart ("Ted" in Chapter 2 of
> *Through the Brick Wall*) Pestrichello,
> director of Casino Administration,
> Tropicana Resort, Las Vegas

"*Through the Brick Wall* provides specific and innovative suggestions and has a seasoning of inspiration and motivation. For anyone who is in, or may be in, the job market, this book would be a good place to start."
> Theodore F. Brophy,
> former chairman of the board, GTE

"A one-woman crusade against unemployment—Kate Wendleton, The Five O'Clock Club, and *Through the Brick Wall!*"
> Roberta Mell,
> vice president, National Advertising,
> Home Box Office

"Harlem adults want to work. We have a high rate of unemployment, and our people often feel hopeless and can see no way out. They feel they are often the last hired and the first fired in times of recession. The Five O'Clock Club is part of the healing process and is helping our people be competitive when they need this kind of help the most."
> Rev. James Russell, III, executive director,
> Harlem YMCA

"Kate is one of the most singularly creative and energetic persons I have ever met. She is completely dedicated to the 'proposition of possibilities' in peoples' lives, and that dedication comes shining through in this book. For those of you not lucky enough to have in person the benefit of Kate's experience, talent, energy and wisdom, *Through the Brick Wall* is the next-best thing to being there."
> Dan Ciporin, vice president, director,
> Worldwide Brand Management,
> major credit card company

"During the time I was looking for a job I kept Kate's book by my bed. I read a little every night, a little every morning. Her common-sense advice, methodical approach, and hints for keeping the spirits up were extremely useful."
> Harold Levine, coordinator,
> Yale Alumni Career Resource Network

"Through the Brick Wall is 'what works now.' This indispensable, no-excuses guide to job-hunting and career building provides a step-by-step approach to organizing your search . . . targeting the job you want . . . getting in for the meetings . . . beating out the competition . . . and turning the interview into an offer."

> Jack Schlegel,
> New York Advertising
> & Communications Network

"Thank you, Kate, for all your help. I ended up with four offers and at least fifteen compliments in two months—all attributed to your work on my résumé. Thanks!"

> president and CEO,
> large banking organization

"I have doubled my salary during the past five years by using The Five O'Clock Club techniques. Now I earn what I deserve. I think everyone needs The Five O'Clock Club and *Through the Brick Wall*."

> M. S., attorney,
> entertainment industry

"I'm an artistic person, and I don't think about business. Kate provided the disciplined business approach so I could practice my art. After adopting her system, I landed a role on Broadway in *Hamlet*."

> Bruce Faulk, actor,
> Manhattan (currently touring Europe in a play)

"Fax to Kate Wendleton: I just got in from Warsaw and am on my way to Prague, but wanted to tell your readers about The Five O'Clock Club and *Through the Brick Wall*. They were directly responsible for the change in my thinking that led to the job I am now enjoying. I would recommend the Club and the book to everyone who needs a new way of looking at things."

> Jessica Burdine, creative director,
> Eastern Europe,
> Grey Düsseldorf

"I love *Through the Brick Wall*, especially the Forty-Year Plan—it helped me see what I should be doing with my life. Without even trying, I have gotten off the treadmill and am working toward my dream. I think everyone should have a Forty-Year Plan, no matter how old they are."

> Milagros Cordero, full-time employee,
> part-time student,
> future teacher and educational filmmaker

"I've heard Kate address audiences many times on the topic of career advancement. *Through the Brick Wall* brings Kate's enthusiastic, thought-provoking style to print. A must-read for every person who has a job, wants one, or may be contemplating changing it."

> Richard Schneyer, chair,
> Career Services Committee, Annual Convention,
> National Society of Fund Raising Executives

THROUGH THE BRICK WALL: HOW TO JOB-HUNT IN A TIGHT MARKET
by KATE WENDLETON (Villard Books)
Book Review by John Reiser,
Director of Group Programs, Right Associates

Kate Wendleton, the founder and driving force of **The Five O'Clock Club**, is a source of amazement to her friends and colleagues, primarily because of her seemingly boundless energy and her relentless optimism ("People are finding jobs!")

That energy and optimism are in evidence throughout Ms. Wendleton's new book *Through the Brick Wall*, but those qualities are only part of what makes *Through the Brick Wall* such an outstanding job-search book.

First, Ms. Wendleton's advice is meticulously correct and universally applicable. There are no gimmicks here; no off-the-wall stunts that might work for an exceptional few but will create only heartache for most job seekers. Second, the advice is complete. Every single stage of the "mating dance" with a potential employer is covered, as are all phases of preparation and of penetrating one's target market.

Perhaps most important, *Through the Brick Wall* is accessible advice. The book will help the most senior executives, squeezed-out middle managers and persons entering the job market for the first time. In fact, every college student on my gift list will get a copy, a largess made possible by the $13.00 price.

All Ms. Wendleton's points are clearly illustrated by actual case studies from among the hundreds of people who have been part of The Five O'Clock Club experience. The genius of this remarkable book is that, while virtually everyone will be able to understand it completely, no one will find it too simplistic. The case studies and the eclectic collection of quotes sprinkled throughout these pages will guarantee that.

Through the Brick Wall should be on every job-search consultant's desk for daily use in identifying and correcting the problems "stuck" candidates present.

Like most career specialists, I try to read enough of the plethora of books on job search to be familiar with what's available. *Through the Brick Wall* is the best book about job search I've ever read.

Through
THE
BRICK
WALL
RÉSUMÉ BUILDER

Kate Wendleton
**author of *Through the Brick Wall:
How to Job-Hunt in a Tight Market***

Five O'Clock Books / New York / 1993

The
Five
O'Clock
Club

Copyright © 1993 by Kate Wendleton and The Five O'Clock Club

Published in the United States by Five O'Clock Books, a division of The Five O'Clock Club, New York.

Some of the contents of this work appeared previously in somewhat different form in *The Job-Changing Workbook, The Five O'Clock News, and Through the Brick Wall: How to Job-Hunt in a Tight Market*

The Five O'Clock Club and Workforce America are registered trademarks.

Library of Congress Cataloging-in-Publication Data

Wendleton, Kate.
    Through the brick wall résumé builder/Kate Wendleton.
        p.   cm.
    Includes index.
    ISBN 0-944054-07-2
    1. Executives—United States.   2. Executives—United States—Supply and demand.
3. Management—Vocational guidance—United States.   4. Job hunting—United States.
5. Career changes—United States.   I. Title
HD38.25.U6W46 1993
650.14'0951—dc20

For information, address The Five O'Clock Club,
1675 York Avenue, 17D, New York, New York 10128

FIRST EDITION
FIRST PRINTING

Manufactured in the United States of America

9 8 7 6 5 4 3 2 1

Dear Reader:

Do you ever feel your résumé isn't representing you in the best way possible? You're probably right. A résumé is not just a recap of what you have done and where. It's a marketing piece that should accurately reflect the way you want a prospective employer to see you.

Studies show that the average résumé is looked at for only ten seconds! So you want a résumé that's scannable so that the reader quickly gets your message. And you not only want a résumé that people look at, you want them to find it so compelling that they look forward to meeting you.

The *Résumé Builder* will take you through the entire process of developing a résumé that's just right for you. We'll make sure you're "positioned" properly for your target market. If your positioning is wrong, your résumé is wrong, and becomes a handicap rather than a help.

This book starts with an overview of The Five O'Clock Club approach to job search. Then we'll work on your accomplishment statements—the backbone of your résumé. We'll teach you the Seven Stories Exercise, which will help you express your accomplishments in a more interesting way. That's just the beginning of how we'll make your résumé more exciting to your reader.

Then we'll work on your summary—the most important and most difficult part of your résumé. Your summary increases your chances of getting exactly the kind of job you want.

Next we'll put it all together by stepping you through lots of sample résumés. The case studies will teach you the nuances of how to *think* about résumé preparation. You'll take your important accomplishments and incorporate them into the body of your résumé, making sure the body supports the statement you created for your summary.

Finally, we'll make sure your résumé is appropriate for your level: we don't want you positioned higher or lower than where you want to be.

Be careful not to simply copy segments of the résumés in this book. ("This one sounds just like me.") It's better to use the most important things from *your* background that you want the hiring manager to know.

This is the best résumé book on the market. It is the only one with case studies. And all the case studies are of actual people. To make the book self-contained, I have included a few excerpts from *Through the Brick Wall* and the *Through the Brick Wall Job Finder*. But if you really want to land that next job, or if you want to think more about your long-term career, be sure to read those books too.

All of this information is based on the highly successful methods used at The Five O'Clock Club®, where the average, regularly attending member finds a job within ten weeks. <u>For a packet of information on joining the Club, call 800-538-6645 ext. 600</u>.

We are guided by the original Five O'Clock Club. The leaders of Old Philadelphia met regularly to exchange ideas and have a good time. Today's members are the same—they exchange ideas, operate at a high level, brainstorm to help each other, and truly enjoy each other's company.

I hope the résumés in this book will give you a feel for some of the wonderful and intriguing people I have met. That's what you want your résumé to do: to entice the reader and make him or her want to meet the author.

I thank the members of The Five O'Clock Club, people who care about their careers. Their hard work is reflected in this book. Thanks to all of our Affiliates in the U.S.A. and Canada. They're committed to bringing the highest-quality career counseling—along with some fun—to those who care. I am most grateful to my editor, Cordelia Jason, for her excellent judgment and apt ideas. She is concerned about every detail, and her suggestions are always on target. Cordelia draws more out of me than I realized I had in me.

Finally, thanks to you for buying this book. Your appreciation of all the years I've spent developing these materials makes it possible for us to continue this effort. Our goal is, and always has been, to provide the best affordable career advice. And, with your help, we will continue to stand by you to help with your career.

Cheers and good luck!

Kate Wendleton
New York City, 1993

The
Five
O'Clock
Club

Table of Contents

Through
THE
BRICK
WALL
RÉSUMÉ BUILDER

I.

OVERVIEW OF THE JOB-SEARCH PROCESS

*You've got to think about "big things"
while you're doing small things,
so that all the small things
go in the right direction.*
Alvin Toffler
Newsweek, April 4, 1988

*The importance of a long-term
perspective cannot be overstated.
It can make the difference between a
career of major contributions and one
characterized by early burnout.
Savvy managers typically seem to have
a longer view than other managers.*
Joel M. DeLuca, Ph.D.
Political Savvy

When most people think of job-hunting, they think "résumé." And certainly a résumé is an important ingredient. After all, I devoted this whole book to résumés! But a résumé is only part of the process that you will see below. What's more, a good résumé is usually the result of a thorough evaluation (or assessment) where you have identified specific job targets (industries and fields), and learned to position yourself to look desirable to hiring managers in those target areas.

On the other hand, you usually need a résumé just to get started in the job-search process—even before you may clearly know the industries or fields you want to target.

It's fine to take a crack at a résumé without going through the assessment—just understand that you have skipped an important step that you should return to later, and that there are several other steps that follow the writing of a résumé.

As your targets become clearer, you may want to revise your résumé to create a better match between you and your targets.

The Job-Search Process

The charts on the following pages outline each part of the process. It's best to do every part, however quickly you may do it. Experienced job hunters pay attention to the details and do not skip a step.

The first part of the process is **assessment** (or evaluation). You evaluate yourself by doing the exercises in *Through the Brick Wall* and the *Through the Brick Wall Job Finder*, and you evaluate your prospects by doing some preliminary research in the library or by talking to people. **Assessment consists of the following exercises**:

- The Seven Stories Exercise
- Interests
- Values

- Satisfiers and Dissatisfiers
- Your Forty-Year Plan

If you are working privately with a career counselor, he or she may ask you to do a few additional exercises, such as a personality test.

Assessment results in:

- a listing of all the targets you think are worth exploring, and
- a résumé that makes you look appropriate to your first target (and may work with other targets as well).

Even if you don't do the entire assessment, the Seven Stories Exercise is especially important because it will help you develop an interesting résumé. Therefore, we have included that exercise in the next chapter.

Research will help you figure out which of your targets:

- are a good fit for you, and
- offer some hope in terms of being a good market.

You can't have too many targets--as long as you rank them. Then, for *each one*, conduct a campaign to get interviews in that target area.

Phase I: Campaign Preparation

- Conduct research to develop a list of all the companies in your first target. Find out the names of the people you should contact in the appropriate departments in each of those companies.
- Develop your cover letter (Paragraph 1 is the opening; Paragraph 2 is a summary about yourself appropriate for this target; Paragraph 3 contains your bulleted accomplishments ("You may be interested in some of the things I've done"); Paragraph 4 is the close. (Lots of sample letters are in the other two books.)
- Develop your plan for getting **lots of interviews in this target**. You have four basic choices:
  - Networking,
  - Direct Contact,
  - Search Firms,
  - Ads.

First say to yourself what you would be;
and then do what you have to do.
Epictetus

You can read lots about each of these methods for getting interviews in both *Through the Brick Wall* and the *Job Finder*.

Phase II : Interviewing

Most people think interviews result in job offers. But there are usually a few intervening steps before a final offer is made. Interviews should result in getting and giving information.

Did you learn the issues important to each person with whom you met? What did they think were your strongest positives? Where are they in the hiring process? How many other people are they considering? How do you compare with those people? Why might they be reluctant to bring you on board, compared with the other candidates? How can you overcome the decision-makers' objections?

This is one of the most important and yet most overlooked parts of the job-search process. It is covered in extensive detail in the other two books.

Phase III: Follow-Up

Now that you have analyzed the interview, you can figure out how to follow up with each person with whom you interviewed. Aim to be following up with six to ten companies. Five job possibilities will fall away through no fault of your own.

What's more, with six to ten things going, you increase your chances of having three good offers to choose from. You would be surprised: even in a tight market, job hunters are able to develop multiple offers.

When you are in the Interview Phase of Target 1, it's time to start Phase I of Target 2. This will give you more momentum and insure that you do not let things dry up. Keep both targets going, and then start Target 3.

Develop Your Unique Résumé

Read all of the case studies in this book. You will learn a powerful new way of thinking about how to position yourself for the kinds of jobs you want. Each of the résumés in this book is for a unique person aiming at a specific target. You and your exact situation are not in here. But seeing how other people position themselves will help you think about what you want a prospective employer to know about you.

After you look at the charts, we'll start gathering important information about you—through the Seven Stories Exercise.

Phases of the Job Search
and the results of each phase:

ASSESSMENT

Consists of:
- The Seven Stories Exercise
- Interests
- Values
- Satisfiers and Dissatisfiers
- Your Forty-Year Plan

Results in:
- As many targets as you can think of
- A ranking of your targets
- A résumé that makes you look appropriate to your first target
- A plan for conducting your search

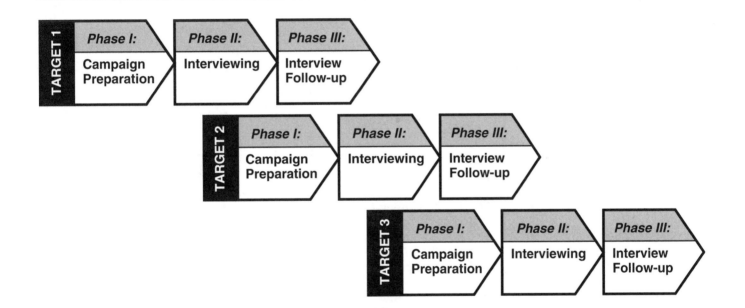

RESULTS

Phase I: Campaign Preparation. *Results in:*	**Phase II: Interviewing.** *Results in:*	**Phase III: Follow-Up.** *Results in:*
❑ Research (list of companies)	❑ Giving them information to keep them interested in you.	❑ Aiming to have 6 to 10 things in the works, and
❑ Résumé	❑ Getting information so you can "move it along."	
❑ Cover Letter		## Job Offers!

❑ Plan for getting interviews
    - *networking*
    - *direct contact*
    - *search firms*
    - *ads*
	❑ Plan for follow-up.
	(You may do several in-depth follow-ups with each person.)	

The
Five
O'Clock
Club®

Getting Interviews;
Building Relationships

Four ways to get interviews in your target market

1. Search Firms
2. Ads
3. Networking
4. Direct Contact:
   - *Targeted Mailing*
   - *Direct Mail Campaign*
   - *Cold Calls*

Plan to contact or meet the *right* people in *every* company in each of your target areas—as quickly as possible.

Get meetings with people in your target areas through:
- Search Firms
- Ads
- Networking
- Direct Contact

Do not think of these as techniques for getting *jobs*, but as techniques for getting *interviews*.

- After a networking meeting, be sure to keep in touch with the person you met.
- After a job interview, think about what you can do next to turn the situation into a job offer.

COMPANIES IN THIS TARGET MARKET	BUILD RELATIONSHIPS	FOLLOW-UP
Company	Contact(s)	
Company	Contact(s)	
Company	Contact(s)	
Company	Contact(s)	
Company	Contact(s)	
Company	Contact(s)	
Company	Contact(s)	
Company	Contact(s)	
and so on ...	Contact(s)	

When you have a meeting, build a relationship: — find out about them; let them know about you.

Figure out how to move each of them along.

II.

ACCOMPLISHMENTS: THE BACKBONE OF YOUR STORY

The Five O'Clock Club

Elizabeth Ghaffari: What a Difference a Story Makes

If you wish in this world to advance,
Your merits you're bound to enhance;
You must stir it and stump it,
And blow your own trumpet,
Or trust me, you haven't a chance.
 William Schwenck Gilbert, *Ruddigore*

Imagination rules the world.
 Napoleon Bonaparte

In differentiation,
not in uniformity,
lies the path of progress.
 Louis Brandeis,
 U.S. Supreme Court Justice,
 Business—A Profession

Every résumé has a pitch—although it may not be what the job hunter wants it to be. In scanning Elizabeth's "before" résumé, we can easily see that she has had communications and advertising positions in a number of computer companies. That's the total extent of her pitch. When she went on interviews, managers commented: "You sure have worked for a lot of computer companies." Her résumé read like a job description: she wrote press releases, product brochures, employee newsletters, and so on.

Thousands of people can write press releases, so citing those skills will not separate Elizabeth from her competition. But we can get to know her better is if she tells us about specific accomplishments.

Elizabeth agreed to do the Seven Stories Exercise. She didn't feel like writing down "the things she enjoyed doing and also did well" because she felt as though she kept doing the same things again and again in every company she worked for, and she enjoyed them all. Still, I urged her to be specific—details can make a résumé more interesting. And working on the stories exercise is a sure way to develop a strong overall message.

She started with an experience on a job early in her career. She had thought of a terrific idea: her company's product could be sold through the same computer systems that were used to sell airline tickets and car and hotel reservations. She convinced the company to let her go ahead with the idea, promoted it to travel agents across the country, and also to the salespeople in her own company. It was so successful, it became the standard way to sell foreign currencies when people were going on a trip.

Most job hunters tend to ignore accomplishments that took place when they were young. But if you had accomplishments early in your career, they may be worth relating because they let the reader know that you have always been a winner.

I said, "That sounds great. Where is it on your résumé?" Elizabeth said: "Well, it's not said exactly that way..." Many times job hunters are constricted when they write their résumés, but the Seven Stories Exercise can free them up to express things differently. So we restated that accomplishment.

Elizabeth then worked on another story. She had participated in a conference that had "generated 450 letters of intent."

I said: "It's nice the conference generated 450 letters of intent. But from what you said, I can't tell that you had anything to do with those results, and I don't know if 450 is good or not. Tell me more about it."

Elizabeth said: "There were only 1500 participants in the conference, and 450 letters of intent is a lot because it's a very expensive product. I had a lot to do with those results because I developed an aura of excitement about the product by putting teasers under everyone's hotel door every morning.

"And before the conference, I had sent five weekly teasers to everyone who planned to attend. For example, one week, I sent each person a bottle of champagne. This direct-mail campaign had everyone talking about us before the convention started. People were asking one another whether or not they had gotten our mailers. When they got to the convention and found teasers under their doors, they were eager to come to our booth.

"I also trained the teams of employees who were demonstrating the product at the convention. I made sure that each demonstrator delivered the same message."

Now I understood how Elizabeth had played a major part in generating those letters of intent.

Next we needed to think of the message behind this accomplishment. Was her message that she could stick mailers under doors? Or send out bottles of champagne? No, her message was that she knew how to launch a product, and that's what we put on her résumé as the main point for that accomplishment.

In her "before" résumé, Elizabeth said that she wrote press releases and did direct-mail campaigns. Her "after" résumé gives us some examples of what she accomplished with those efforts, and gives us a feel for her ingenuity and hard work.

The Summary

After we reviewed all of her accomplishments, we tackled the summary. What was the most important point Elizabeth wanted to get across? It wasn't just that she could write press releases and speeches, or do direct-mail campaigns.

She had to think hard about this. The most important thing was that Elizabeth was a key member of the management team. She sat in on meetings when the company was discussing bringing out a new product, or planning how to handle a possible crisis. Elizabeth would not be happy—or effective—in a job where she simply wrote press releases. She needed to be part of the strategy sessions.

What you put on your résumé can both include you and exclude you. A company that does not want the communications person included in those meetings would not be interested in Elizabeth—but then, she wouldn't be interested in them either.

In her summary, instead of highlighting the companies she had worked for, Elizabeth highlighted the industries represented by those companies. She listed Information Services and High-Tech first, because they represented areas of greater growth than Financial Services did.

Elizabeth was—and wanted to be again—a corporate strategist, a crisis manager, and a spokesperson for the corporation. That's how we positioned her.

In every summary in this book (and in *Through the Brick Wall*), the reader can tell something about the writer's personality. It is not enough that someone knows what you have done, they also need to know your style in doing it. For example, a person who had run a department and doubled productivity could have done it in a nasty, threatening way, or could have motivated people to do more, instituted training programs, and encouraged workers to come up with suggestions for improving productivity. Your style matters.

Look at this case study and then do the Seven Stories Exercise. Come up with accomplishments that will interest your reader. Let him or her know what to expect from you if you are hired.

In Elizabeth's case, we hope the hiring manager will look at her résumé and say: "That's exactly what I need: a corporate strategist who knows how to handle crises, and can also serve as a spokesperson for us."

This is the response you want the reader to have: "That's exactly the person I need!" Look at your résumé. What words pop out? Is this how you want to be seen? If not, let's get going.

After you have worked hard on your résumé, use your summary to develop your brief verbal pitch to be used in interviews and the summary statement in your cover letters. You will see lots of examples of these in both *Through the Brick Wall* and the *Job Finder*.

QUOTES TO INSPIRE YOU

Image can be true, false, or in between, but until you have one, for the world of the movies you don't exist.
Michael Caine, *Acting in Film*

Man simply conforms. Many people feel they are powerless to do anything effective with their lives. It takes courage to break out of the settled mold, but most find conformity more comfortable. That is why the opposite of courage in our society is not cowardice—it's conformity.
Rollo May

All that is needed is a plan, a road map, and the courage to press on to your destination. You must know in advance that there will be disappointments and setbacks—but you must also know that nothing on earth can stand in the way of a well-thought-out plan backed by persistence and determination.
Dennis Kimbro,
Think and Grow Rich: A Black Choice

While you can think in terms of efficiency in dealing with time, a principle-centered person thinks in terms of effectiveness in dealing with people.
Stephen R. Covey,
The Seven Habits of Highly Effective People

We are prone to judge success by the index of our salaries or the size of our automobiles rather than by the quality of our service and relationship to humanity.
Martin Luther King, Jr.

ELIZABETH GHAFFARI

207 Dobbs Ferry
Phoenix, AZ 44444

Home: (609) 555-6666

EXPERIENCE

ORANGE COMPUTER SYSTEMS
Director Corporate Communications

1988 - Present

Plan and supervise all corporate communications staff and activities for diversified financial information services company on a global basis.

- Develop, direct and implement global media, public relations, and internal-communications programs in support of corporate and sales objectives, working closely with executive management team.

- Direct all media-relations activities related to new product introductions and product enhancements; initiate media contacts; respond to press inquiries; coordinate and conduct interviews; and develop all press materials.

- Develop and direct advertising and promotional literature activities, overseeing all corporate publications, including corporate and product brochures, sales materials, and customer and employee newsletters.

ELECTRONIC DATA SYSTEMS
Manager, Advertising and Promotion

1986 - 1988

Developed and implemented marketing and promotion strategies for Reuters and its North American subsidiaries.

- Worked with market and product managers to identify opportunities for product and sales promotions and new product development for multiple market segments. Conducted market research, developed marketing strategies and implemented tactical plans (e.g. direct response marketing and sales incentive programs).

- Responsible for planning biannual securities analyst meetings and communication product information to investors and industry analysts.

- Orchestrated six product introductions during three-month period, including public-relations activities, promotional literature and training materials.

- Responsible for forecasting and maintaining $4.0 million budget.

- Managed corporate and product advertising programs, hiring and working with various agencies.

CREDIT LYONNAIS   1984 - 1986
Corporate Investment Officer and Product Manager

Planned and directed the sales and promotion efforts for the bank's corporate and correspondent sales staff for a variety of products including foreign exchange and precious metals.

- Developed active and profitable business relationships with correspondent banks for sale of precious metals and foreign exchange products.

- Established and developed new account relationships. Brought in eleven new corporate accounts which produced significant business in precious metals and foreign exchange trading areas.

- Managed market study to identify size, segments and opportunities of various markets. Prepared analysis and recommendations for new product development and trading vehicles.

WASSERELLA & BECKTON   1979 - 1984
Director of Marketing

Managed all activities of the Marketing Department, including product development, sales promotion, advertising and public relations activities for diversified financial services company.

- Conceptualized and developed national marketing strategy for foreign exchange services offered to travel industry professionals via automated airline reservation systems.

- Developed and implemented business plans for a variety of products, including responsibility for product positioning, pricing, contracts, advertising and promotional materials.

- Promoted from Foreign Exchange Trader to Marketing Representative to Director of Marketing in three years.

EDUCATION

B.A., Psychology, University of Phoenix   1979

ELIZABETH GHAFFARI

207 Dobbs Ferry
Phoenix, AZ 44444

Residence: (609) 555-6666
Work: (493) 345-7777

CORPORATE COMMUNICATIONS EXECUTIVE
with 14 years' experience in

- **High-Tech**   • **Information Services**   • **Financial Services**

Experience includes:

- Global Media and Investor Relations
- Customer Videos and Newsletters
- Advertising/Promotional Literature
- Employee Newsletters
- Employee Roundtables/Awards Programs
- Speech-Writing/Papers/Public Speaking

- <u>**A corporate strategist and key member of the management team**</u> with extensive knowledge of financial markets.

- <u>**A crisis manager**</u>: bringing common sense, organizational skills, and a logical decision-making process to solving sensitive, time-critical problems.

- <u>**A spokesperson for the corporation**</u>: developing and communicating key corporate messages accurately and convincingly, under deadline pressure, to multiple audiences including employees, the media, customers and investors.

**Proven team leader and problem solver with highly developed
analytical, organizational, communications, and strategic planning skills.**

ORANGE COMPUTER SYSTEMS   1988 - Present

<u>Director, Corporate Communications</u>

- Gained extensive positive media coverage in conjunction with launch of company's first product for new market segment.
  - Planned and conducted **media events in 8 countries**.
  - Resulted in **positive stories in 30 major publications** and trade press: *The Wall Street Journal, The New York Times, Barron's, The Financial Times, Forbes,* and various foreign publications.
  - A first for the company, **positive TV coverage in the United States**: CNN, CNBC, **and Europe**: Sky Financial Television, Business Daily, The City Programme.

- Successfully **avoided communications crisis**, gained positive press coverage and customer support when company sold a major division. Within a 60-day period:
  - Planned and managed all aspects of a **13-city, interactive teleconference**.
  - Developed all written materials including various employee and customer communications, background materials and press releases.
  - Wrote speeches for six executives including both company presidents (present and acquiring companies).
  - Wrote and produced an extensive question-and-answer document covering **union, compensation and benefits issues and business rational.**
  - Selected and trained staff representatives for each of 13 cities.

ORANGE COMPUTER SYSTEMS, contd.
Director, Corporate Communications, contd.

- Developed and implemented **company's first employee awards program** for service excellence.
  - Honored employees who participated in planning sessions.
  - **Led to changes in key areas** including improvements in software manufacturing efficiencies, shortening of the product development cycle, and improved employee morale.

- **Introduced desk-top publishing** program for in-house production of all promotional materials and various customer and employee newsletters.
  - **Reduced outside services expense by 75%.**
  - Created new **corporate standards manual** and reorganized promotional literature system to replace inconsistent product literature.

- Conducted group and individual **employee meetings** to gain and disseminate critical information in identifying and resolving employee-relations problems.

- Prepared quarterly management reports and written/oral presentations to top management and employees to describe corporate accomplishments compared to goals.

- Managed all customer/media/employee communications for sale of three business units.

ELECTRONIC DATA SYSTEMS   1986 - 1988
Manager, Advertising and Promotion

- Prepared written and oral **presentations to boards of directors** and senior managers on various services, concepts and results.

- Planned **product launch** and company participation in global foreign exchange conference. Successful product launch resulted in **generating 450 letters of intent from 1500 participants.** Assured successful product introduction:
  - Developed 5-week **direct-mail campaign** to stimulate interest and create an aura of excitement around product prior to conference. Campaign continued at conference with daily newsletter and door stuffer.
  - Maximized impact of **product demonstrations** through use of compelling visual presentation and environment.
  - **Trained teams** of product demonstrators to assure that information regarding benefits and features would be delivered in consistent way.

- Strengthened company relationships with **industry analysts and investors** by arranging product demonstrations in conjunction with bi-annual industry analyst meetings. Demonstrations stimulated interest and **gained support for strategic direction from investor community** by communicating important strategic and product information.
  - Selected products to be demonstrated, developed promotional materials, organized display area, selected and trained product demonstrators to assure delivery of consistent corporate message.

CREDIT LYONNAIS   1984 - 1986
Product Manager

- Established and developed new account relationships.
  - Brought in **11 new corporate accounts during 10-month period** producing significant business in precious metals and foreign exchange trading areas.

WASSERELLA & BECKTON   1979 - 1984
Director of Marketing

- **Developed breakthrough idea to sell** foreign exchange services (currency and travelers' checks) through travel agents the same way hotel space and airline tickets are sold
  — **via automated airline reservation systems**.
  - Sold concept to senior management and **negotiated contracts with three major airlines**.
  - Developed sales and operational procedures. **Hired and trained 10-person sales and operations staff.**
  - **Promoted concept to travel agents** across the country through industry trade shows and sales program.

EDUCATION

B.A., Psychology, University of Phoenix, 1979

The Seven Stories Exercise

This exercise is an opportunity to examine the most satisfying experiences of your life and to discover those skills you will want to use as you go forward. You will be looking at the times when you feel you did something particularly well that you also enjoyed doing. It doesn't matter what other people thought, whether or not you were paid, or when in your life the experiences took place. **All that matters is that you felt happy about doing whatever it was, thought you did it well, and experienced a sense of accomplishment.** You can even go back to childhood. When I did my own Seven Stories Exercise, I remembered the time when I was ten years old and led a group of kids in the neighborhood, enjoyed it, and did it well. If you need more ideas, consult Chapter 7 of *Through the Brick Wall*.

This exercise usually takes a few days to complete. Many people review different life phases in order to capture the full scope of these experiences. You might want to carry around a piece of paper to jot down ideas as you think of them.

SECTION I:

Briefly outline below *all* the work/personal/life experiences which meet the above definition. Keep going until you come up with at least twenty. We ask for twenty stories so you won't be too selective. Just write down anything that occurs to you, no matter how trivial it may seem. Try to **think of concrete examples, situations and tasks, not generalized skills or abilities**. It may be helpful if you say to yourself, "There was the time when I . . . "

RIGHT	WRONG
• Got extensive media coverage for a new product launch.	• Writing press releases.
• Delivered speech to get German business.	• Delivering speeches.
• Coordinated blood drive for division.	• Coordinating.
• Came in third in the Nassau Bike Race.	• Cycling.
• Made a basket in second grade.	• Working on projects alone.

1. _____

2. _____

3. _____

4. _____

5. _____

6. _____

7. _____

8. _____

9. _____

10. _____

11. _____

12. _____

13. _____

which you enjoyed the most and felt the most sense of accomplishment
riences also.) Then **rank them**. Then, for each accomplishment, describe
ach step in detail. Notice the role you played and your relationship with
u used, and so on. Use a separate sheet of paper for each.
lso happen to be work-related, you may want them to appear prominently
that you enjoyed and did well. And those are probably the experiences you

at resulted in 450 letters of intent from 1500 participants.

managers to discuss product potential and details.

b. Developed promotional plan.

c. Conducted five-week direct-mail campaign prior to the conference to create an aura of excitement about the product.

d. Trained all product demonstrators to make sure they each presented our product in the same way.

e. Had a great product booth built; rented the best suite to entertain prospects; conducted campaign at the conference by having teasers put under everyone's door every day of the conference. Most people wanted to come to our booth.

—and so on—

People cannot let others limit their imagination of what it is they want to do or can do. Otherwise, we would never have discoveries or advance.
Mae C. Jemison, physician, chemical engineer, and
America's first black woman astronaut

Action may not always bring happiness, but there is no happiness without action.
Benjamin Disraeli

In the next section, we'll polish up your accomplishments.

After that, we'll help you with your summary statement, which goes at the top of your résumé. It's the most important thing your reader will see, and it is also the most difficult part to do well. That's okay. You will have lots of summary statements to look at, so you will be able to develop one that is right for you.

Finally, we'll put it all together by looking at the Résumé Case Studies. They will help you understand the thinking and the strategy that go into a really great résumé.

How to State Your Accomplishments

Start where you are with what you have,
knowing that what you have
is plenty enough.
Booker T. Washington

Your accomplishments form the backbone of your résumé. Accomplishment statements are short, measurable, and results-oriented.

You may want to start with your most important story from the Seven Stories Exercise--if it was work-related. Polish up that accomplishment, and a few more. If you want your reader to know about these accomplishments, work hard to state them correctly. When you have finished refining three or four major accomplishments, you'll be surprised by how much of your résumé is already done.

Alternatively, start with your most recent position. State your title, company name, and list your accomplishments. Rather than ranking them chronologically (First I did this, and then I did that . . .), rank them in the order of interest to the reader.

After refining the accomplishment statements for your present or most recent position, examine the job before that one. State your title, your company name, and list your accomplishments.

You will feel more hopeful about your job search after you have completed this exercise. Your accomplishments will be stated in a way that will make you proud.

Also consider your accomplishments outside work. These too should be short, measurable, and results-oriented. By doing volunteer work after-hours, many have gained experiences that helped them move from their current fields into new ones.

Here are a few accomplishment statements from various professionals. They are written in the context of a complete job so you can see how to bullet and sub-bullet. This technique of bulleting and sub-bulleting can be used on any person's résumé.

VICE PRESIDENT OF MARKETING SERVICES   1985-1987

- Contributed to 3 consecutive years of record 9.7% growth.

- Developed marketing and sales **training programs for 5,000 employees**.

  - Program changed "hard sell"/reactive selling to consultative and entrepreneurial approach.

  - Program shifted selling culture and positioned company for growth in the 80's.

- **Repositioned subsidiary** by redesigning logo, signage, brochures, direct-mail solicitations, and collateral materials.

- Introduced customer-satisfaction measurement program that provided feedback to 1,100 branch operations and produced changes in operational procedures.

This example is written the way it would appear on a résumé. Note that certain parts are underlined so the reader cannot miss them. It makes the résumé more scannable.

If you want the reader to know that you have developed training programs, does it hit the reader's eye? If you are proud of having repositioned a subsidiary and think it may be important to your next employer, can he find it on your résumé? You will not have to think about highlighting your résumé until it is completely put together. For now, just know that it will be an option later. The following pages contain sample accomplishments.

International Rescue Committee, Sakaeo, Thailand 　　1980-1981
Educational Programs Coordinator

Directed all educational programs in Thailand's second-largest Cambodian refugee camp, with a population of 35,000.

- Managed a budget of $300,000 and an international staff of 550.

- Conceived of and introduced programs which resulted in both a 250% expansion of participants and national recognition.

- Negotiated regularly with the Thai Government and the United Nations.

Depending on the positions he is going after, these accomplishments may be included or not. They may, for example, be unimportant for ten years, and later on become important again, depending on his job target.

Vice President, Chief Budget Officer 　　1988-1989
Major Not-for-Profit

Reported to Chief Financial Officer. Staff of 50 in two cities. Joined management team of new CEO and CFO to implement a more results-oriented culture in a non-profit environment.

- Coordinated annual corporate budget of $500 million expenses.
  - Introduced top-down approach, PC modeling and budget programs.

- Developed cost-allocation computer system to transfer over $200 million in indirect back-office expenses.

- Projected program costs, including . . .
  - Correcting cost allocations to collect over $2 million in additional annual revenues.
  - Saving program $3 million in potential cost overruns.
  - Developing product costs for future programs, as a member of product-development teams.

- Improved financial systems and information flow:
  - Streamlined financial reporting, **reduced cycle by 5 days**.
  - Presented strategic plan to upgrade financial systems.

Her job was basically a process-oriented job: getting things to run smoothly, reducing the reporting cycle. Process-oriented jobs can still be presented in terms of accomplishments.

Curator, Penobscott Museum 　　1971 - 1974

Organized all major exhibitions (5 to 6 per year) and their accompanying catalogues.

- Developed educational programs supplementing these exhibitions.
- Reorganized Museum's collection of paintings, sculptures and graphics.
- Organized special films, concerts and lectures at Museum.
- Maintained an extensive speaking schedule; promoted public relations.
- Supervised the activities of curatorial, library and installation assistants.

Senior Paralegal   **1980 - 1988**
Burstein, Kleinder and Feld, PC

- Trained, directed and **supervised four support employees**.
- Administered, coordinated and ran secured-loan transactions.
- Served as liaison to clients and attorneys; wrote detailed progress reports.

Office Manager/Chiropractic Assistant   **1986 - 1989**
Dr. James Taylor

One-person office force for this busy chiropractic office.
- Transcribed own correspondence.
- Set up Leading Edge Word Processor.
- Assisted doctor with exam preparation.
- Billed patients, maintained patient files, answered phones, ordered medical and office supplies, handled appointments.

Brevard Elementary School, Parent Volunteer   1984 - 1993

- Assisted teachers with proofreading/grading students' creative writing assignments.
- Coordinated/edited newspapers for two class groups.

Her volunteer work shows that she has the experience necessary to do that next job.

Federated Department Stores Atlanta, GA.
Sales Assistant, Summer 1984

- Sold merchandise in various departments and resolved complaints.
- Balanced daily accounts and prepared displays.

Summer jobs can count too.

Editor/Public Relations Manager, Outboard Marine   1968-1969

- Edited company magazine and handled company P.R. duties.
- Obtained publicity through most national trade magazines.
- Coordinated free-lance artists and writers around the country in producing special on-the-spot application stories about the company's products.
- Distributed innovative ideas and encouragement/promotional letters to dealers.
- Attended meetings and conventions.
- Assisted in advertising campaigns, such as photography of products.

Although he held this job a long time ago, the details are important to what this career-changer wants to do next.

Polish up your accomplishment statements.

Rework the wording of your accomplishments. Think how they will sound to the reader. Do not "tell all." Make the reader want to meet you to find out more.

In addition, rephrase your accomplishments to make them as independent as possible of the particular environment you were working in. Make your accomplishments seem useful in other companies or even other industries.

Here is an accomplishment statement as originally written:

> **Compared the changes in various categories of revenue to the changes in various categories of labor. Plotted results on a scatter diagram to show the relationships.**

That is so boring. What were you really doing and why? Look at what you did as if you were an observer rather than the grunt working on something day in and day out. What were the results of your efforts?

Here is that same accomplishment statement reworked:

> **Defined the factors that influence profitability in professional service firms. Resulted in launch of major reorganization of company's largest division.**

Sounds better, doesn't it? The first example sounds like a person who is technical and adds up numbers all day—which is what this project was. The rewrite sounds like a person who knew what he or she was doing, had some say in how it was done, and was aware of the impact on the organization— perhaps even pushed for the changes that took place in the company. The new wording makes the reader want to meet this person to learn new insights.

Here is another "before-and-after" example. The first one was not bad:

Investor Business Manager,   **1986 - 1987**
Middle East, Africa Division

- **Reinvigorated risk-taking; improved credit practices** during rebuilding of business in Gulf region. Managed relationships with selected investors.

- Helped **modernize and strengthen risk management** in various functions of the European division. Led a group critique of risk-management issues.

In the re-write, the job hunter thought more about what he *really* did in the job. That became the main focus, with the details subordinate to that.

Manager, Middle East Investor Business,   1986 - 1987
Middle East, Africa Division

Redefined the opportunities in and helped rebuild Gulf Region business after years during which the company perceived high risks and low profit- ability. Had operating centers in 5 countries, 400+ staff.

- **Redirected marketing** to focus on clients' needs as investors.
- **Reinvigorated risk-taking** <u>and</u> improved credit practices.
- **Improved profitability.**
- Designated a **senior credit officer** and division risk manager.

When writing your accomplishments:

• *Focus on results,* as opposed to the process you went through. Focus on the effect your actions had.

• *Use quantitative measures* when possible. If the quantity doesn't sound important, don't use it.

• *Show the part you played* in whatever happened to your company. If the company grew from $50 million to $200 million, were you an observer or did you have something to do with it? What was your key accomplishment?

• Don't say what you did. *State the magnitude and the effect* it had. For example, if you say you "started up a new computer system," that statement could apply to anyone at any level. What effect did that computer system have on the company? Rework your accomplishment to say:

Developed spreadsheet program to highlight salary inconsistencies within range. Resulted in a more equitable personnel system and savings of $100,000 a year.
or:
Solely responsible for the development of a computerized system that resulted in a new way to analyze accounts. Resulted in $2-million profit improvement and the renegotiation of key accounts.

Now go back and rework *your* accomplishment statements.

Other areas to list:

Skills and equipment. If you are in a technical job, you may want to list the equipment you are familiar with, such as computers or computer languages or software, and perhaps foreign languages you know.

Books or articles written; speeches delivered. One important example implies you have done more. If you have addressed the United Nations, do not mention the speech you gave at a neighborhood meeting.

Organizations. List organizations related to the work you are seeking. If you list too many, the reader may wonder how you will have time for work.

How you will use your accomplishments list

Your list of key accomplishments will help you interview, write cover letters, and prepare your résumé. It is the raw material for the rest of your job hunt.

These are the key selling points about you—the things that will make you different from your competition. They will also whet the appetite of the reader, so he or she will want to meet you. The purpose of a résumé or cover letter is not to tell what you did, but to get interviews. During the interview, you can elaborate on what you did.

Figuring out what you really did is much more difficult than simply reciting your job description. That's the importance of doing the Seven Stories Exercise. It helps you step back from a résumé frame-of-mind so you can concentrate on the most important accomplishments of your life (in terms of what you really enjoyed doing and know you also did well). Then the exercise helps you to think about each accomplishment in terms of what led up to it, what your role was, what gave you satisfaction, what your motivation was, and so on.

When you write your accomplishments, think about your future and those parts of your accomplishments you may want to emphasize, and think about what you *really* did.

If you think you haven't done a thing with your life

Many people are intimidated when they see other people's accomplishments. They think they have none of their own. Chances are, you aren't thinking hard enough about what you have done. Even obviously accomplished people struggle to express what they have done.

If you think you haven't done much, think again. Even the lowest-level clerks have accomplishments they are proud of. At all levels in an organization, people can be presented with problems and figure out how to handle them.

Don't compare yourself with others, and don't worry about what your boss or peers thought of what you did. Maybe they did not appreciate your talents. Brag about what you have done anyway—even though your boss may have taken credit for the work you did, and even though you may have done it with others. Think of problems you have faced in your company. What did you do to handle them? What was the result for your company? Think of an accomplishment. Write it down. Then pare it down until you can show the reader what you handled and the impact it made.

Finally, don't say anything negative about yourself. Don't lie, but don't hurt yourself either. For example, never lie about where you got a degree or whether you got a degree. If you are found out, you will be fired. If you have been unemployed for a very long time, see my specific hints on how to discuss this awkward timeframe in Chapter 24 of *Through the Brick Wall.*

In the next chapter, we will prepare the summary for your résumé, and then help you to put it all together.

The
Five
O'Clock
Club®

III.

POSITIONING YOURSELF

Positioning Power for a Job Change

Feel stuck in your present position? Peel off your old label, slap on a new one, and position yourself for something different.

Whether you're a branch manager who wants to go into commercial lending, or an operations person who dreams of being a trainer, the challenge you face is the same: you have to convince people that, even though you don't have experience, you can handle the new position.

It's a little like show biz: you play the same role for years and then you get typecast. It can be difficult for people to believe that you can play a different role. To move on to new challenges, you have to negotiate into the new job by offering seemingly unrelated skills as an added benefit to the employer. The key to these negotiations is "positioning" yourself.

Positioning

Simply put, positioning yourself means stating your skills and qualities in a way that makes it easy for the prospective employer to see you in the position that is open or in other positions down the road.

You may want to stay in your present company. In that case, you are positioning yourself to the person in charge of hiring for the particular department you want to enter. Or, you may want to go to a new company or even a new industry. In this case, you are positioning yourself to a new employer. Either way, the steps are the same:

1) Decide what skills and qualities your prospective employer wants.

2) Search your background to see where you have demonstrated skills that would apply.

3) Write a "position statement" and use it as the basis for your résumé.

4) Use the position statement to sell yourself in an interview.

Your position statement says it all. It should sell your ability, experience, and personality. It brings together all your accomplishments.

The rest of your résumé should support the position statement. For example, if the statement says that you're a financial wizard, the résumé had better support that. It's completely within your control to tell whatever story you want to tell. You can emphasize certain parts of your background and deemphasize others.

> **You can get typecast. To move on, you have to negotiate into the new job . . . by "positioning" yourself.**

Thinking through your position statement is not easy, but it focuses your entire job hunt. It forces you to clarify the sales pitch you will use in interviews.

However, a position statement is *not* what many people put on their résumés. They say they want "a challenging job in a progressive and growth-oriented company that uses all my strengths and abilities." That doesn't say anything at all, and it doesn't do you any good.

Let's consider a few examples of statements that *will* work for you:

Pursuing the Dream Job

Jane, a client-relationship manager at a major bank, has handled high-net-worth clients for more than twenty years. She is taking early retirement and thinking about a second career. Two directions interest her: one, a job similar to what she has done but in a smaller bank; or, the job of her dreams—working as one of the top administrative people for a high-net-worth family (such as the Rockefellers), handling their business office and perhaps doing some of the things that involve her hobbies over the years: staffing and decorating.

If Jane were to continue on her current career path and go for a position as a relationship manager at a smaller bank, she would highlight the years she has worked at the bank. Her position statement, if used in her résumé, would look like this:

Over 20 years handling all aspects of fiduciary relationships for Premier-Bank's private banking clients. Successfully increased revenue through new business efforts, client cultivation, and account assessment. Consistently achieved fee increases. Received regular bonus awards.

However, to pursue her "dream" job, Jane's regular résumé won't do. She has to "reposition" herself to show that her experience fits what her prospective employer needs. Her position statement would read like this:

Administrative manager with broad experience in running operations. In-depth work with accountants, lawyers, agents, and so on. Over 20 years' experience handling all aspects of fiduciary relationships for PremierBank's private banking clients (overall net worth of $800 million). Expert in all financial arrangements (trust and estate accounts, asset management, non-profit, and tenant shareholder negotiations).

Her résumé would focus on her work *outside* of PremierBank because these activities would interest her prospective employer: first, her work with the high-class apartment building of which she was president for fourteen years, and then the post she held for ten years as treasurer of a nonprofit organization. Finally, Jane would highlight the work she had done at PremierBank that would be of interest to her prospective employer, such as the account on which she saved a client $300,000 in taxes.

Ready to Take Charge

Robert had worked in every area of benefits administration. Now he would like to head up the entire benefits administration area—a move to management. His positioning statement:

14 years' experience in design and administration of all areas of employee benefit plans, including five years with Borgash Benefits Consultants. Advised some of the largest and most prestigious companies in the country. Excellent training and communications skills. MBA in Finance. An effective manager who delivers consistent results.

From Supporting to Selling

Jack wants to move into sales after being in marketing support. He has been an executive in the sales promotion area, so his position statement stresses his marketing as well as his management experience:

10 years' progressive marketing and managerial experience. Devise superior marketing strategies through qualitative analysis and product repositioning. Skillful at completing the difficult internal sale, coupled with the ability to attract business and retain clients. Built strong relationships with the top consulting firms. A team player with an enthusiastic approach to top-level challenges.

Notice how he packages his experience running a marketing department as sales. His pitch will be, "It's even more difficult to sell inside because, in order to keep my job, I have to get other people in my company to use my marketing services. I have to do a good job, or they won't use me again."

Jack lacked a position statement on former résumés. If you do not have a position statement, then your position, by default, is the last position you held. With this statement, however, the employer would receive the résumé and say, "Ah-ha! Just what we need—a salesperson!"

Making a Career Change

Elliott had been in sports marketing years ago, and had enjoyed it tremendously. However, he had spent the past four years in the mortgage industry, and was having a hard time getting back into sports marketing.

The sports people saw him as a career changer—and they saw him as an mortgage man. Even when he explained that marketing mortgages is the same as marketing sports, people did not believe him. He was being positioned by his most recent experience, which was handicapping him.

When a job hunter wants to change industries—or go back to an old industry—he cannot let his most recent position act as a handicap. For example, if a person has always been in pharmaceuticals marketing, and now wants to do marketing in another industry, the résumé should be rewritten to make it generic marketing, and most references to pharmaceuticals should be removed.

In Elliott's case, the summary in the new résumé helps a great deal to bring his old work experience right to the top of the résumé. In addition, Elliott has removed the word "mortgage" from the description of his most recent job, his title at the mortgage company now stands out more than the company name, and he has gotten rid of company and industry jargon, such as the job title of segment director, because it is not something easily understood outside of his company.

Industry is a better horse to ride than genius.
Walter Lippmann

Elliott Jones

421 Morton Street   Chase Fortune, KY 23097

Sears Mortgage Company   **1987 - present**
Vice President, Segment Director, Shelter Business
- Director of $4.6-billion residential-mortgage business for the largest mortgage lender in the nation.
- Organized and established regional marketing division for largest mortgage lender in nation, a business which included first and second mortgages, and mortgage life insurance.

SportsLife Magazine   1985 - 1987
Publisher and Editor
- Published and edited the largest consumer health and fitness magazine and increased circulation 175%.

and so on. . .

Elliott Jones

421 Morton Street   Chase Fortune, KY 23097

Summary of Qualifications

Fifteen-plus years of domestic and international senior management experience in the **leisure/sporting goods industry**; multi-brand expertise specializing in marketing, new business development, strategic planning, and market research.

Proven record of identifying customer segments, developing differentiable product platforms, communication strategies, sales management, share growth, and profit generation.

Business Experience

Sears Mortgage Company   1987 - present
VICE PRESIDENT, BUSINESS DIRECTOR
Residential Real Estate Business

- Business Director of a $4.6-billion business. Managed strategic planning, marketing, product development, and compliance.

- Consolidated four regional business entities into one; doubled product offerings. Grew market share 150 basis points and solidified #1 market position.

- Developed and executed nationally recognized consumer and trade advertising, public relations, and direct-response programs.

- Structured a product development process which integrated product introductions into the operations and sales segments of the business.

- Organized and established regional marketing division for largest mortgage lender in nation, a business which included first and second mortgages, and mortgage life insurance.

SPORTSLIFE MAGAZINE   1985 - 1987
Publisher and Editor

- Published and edited the largest consumer health and fitness magazine and increased circulation 175%.
and so on. . .

Notice that the description of what Elliott did for the mortgage business is now written generically—it can apply to the marketing of *any* product. With his new résumé, Elliott had no trouble speaking to people in the sports industry. They no longer saw his most recent experience as a handicap, and he soon had a terrific job as head of marketing for a prestigious sporting-goods company.

If you want to move into a new industry or profession, state what you did generically so people will not see you as tied to the old.

Bring Something to the Party

When it comes down to negotiating yourself into a new position, seemingly unrelated skills from former positions may actually help you get the job.

For example, some of my background had been in accounting and computers when I decided to go into counseling. My CFO experience helped me ease into that career. I applied at a ninety-person career counseling company and agreed to be their CFO for a while—provided I was also assigned clients to counsel. They wanted a cost-accounting system, so my ability to do that for them was what I "brought to the party." I was willing to give the company something they wanted (my business experience) in ex-

change for doing something I really wanted to do (counseling executives).

Combining the new with the old, rather than jumping feet first into something completely new, is often the best way to move your career in a different direction. You gain the experience you need in the new field without having to enter at the entry level. Equally important, it is less stressful because you are using some of your old strengths while you build new ones.

Coming from a background different from the field you are targeting can also give you a bargaining chip. If you are looking at an area where you have no experience, you will almost certainly be competing with people who do have experience. You can separate yourself from the competition by saying, "I'm different. I have the skills to do this job, and I can also do other things that these people can't do." It works!

In the sample résumés in this book, you will see how the positioning statements are used to set the tone for the rest of the résumé.

Additional positioning (summary) statements can be found on the following pages and in Chapter 10 of *Through the Brick Wall.*

*I know what pleasure is,
for I have done good work.*
Robert Louis Stevenson

Don't forget that it (your product or service) is not differentiated until the customer understands the difference.
Tom Peters, *Thriving on Chaos*

What are the most important points you want your target market to know about you? Say them in your summary. Take a look at the positioning statements here and in *Through the Brick Wall*.

Try not to be too intimidated by the summaries you read here. You are seeing people with their best foot forward. They may have struggled for hours to come up with these summa-ries. Don't be discouraged. Remember that this is the most difficult part of the résumé to write, but it is also the most important. Try it, and see how well you can show off what you have done.

And be sure to look at the summaries in the résumé section of this book. Plenty more are there, many with "before" résumés--the initial attempts people made.

---

15 years' experience as a clerk at J.C. Penney's. Stock shelves. Fill out documents. Pay attention to all details. Excellent attendance. Show up on time. Personable and pitch in to help others.

Summary of Qualifications

<u>Over 2 years' experience in PC Development and Support</u>. Support and advise senior management on computer needs and implementation. <u>Experience in all areas of project management</u>. Work well with people with varying computer abilities. Take initiative. Place high value on accuracy.

Summary of Qualifications

An honors degree in Marketing (<u>magna cum laude</u>) is coupled with <u>four years of professional marketing experience</u> and a solid history of <u>successful projects, promotions and awards</u>. Ability to coordinate the efforts of many to meet organizational goals. High in energy, with strong interpersonal skills.

Professional Skills

Hands-on experience within Marketing includes: Market Research, Marketing Support, Project Management, Public Speaking, Training, Computers and Vendor relations.

SUMMARY OF QUALIFICATIONS

Planning and policy professional with experience in <u>international and government affairs</u>. Planned and prescribed courses of action to achieve the objectives of <u>corporate, government, and non-profit organizations</u>. Developed policies for company's domestic and foreign businesses. Well-rounded individual with a demonstrated ability to work effectively in a variety of environments and cultures. Excellent research, communications, and interpersonal skills.

Four years of executive secretarial experience coupled with continuing college education. A solid history of excellent work relationships, both with the public and with internal personnel at all organizational levels. High in initiative and energy with strong ability to exercise independent judgment. Excellent writing skills. Trustworthy and discreet.

Professional Experience

Typing Speed: 75-80 wpm   Shorthand Speed: 95-100 wpm
Qualified to operate all standard business equipment, including word processsors

But more importantly, can take on major projects and handle from initiation and planning through to implementation and follow-up.

Summary of Qualifications

A podiatrist in private practice.
A reputation for being professional, courteous and knowledgeable about state-of-the-art treatment modalities.

- Give my best to both project and patient.
- Set high standards. Thorough and detail-oriented.
- Build **excellent rapport with colleagues and patients** alike.
- Superior oral and written skills.
- From a family of doctors.
- Member, **Board of Directors**, American Red Cross, South Central L.A. Service Center

---

Experienced television journalist
with both national and international experience.

- **60 MINUTES**   • **VISNEWS LIMITED**   • **CHARLIE ROSE**   • **THE FORD FOUNDATION**

Particular expertise in:

- Proposal drafting and presentation for special events and projects.
- Coverage of Capitol Hill and White House news events.
- Newsgathering, packaging and editing.
- International satellite feed coordination.

Fluent in English and Portuguese with working knowledge of Spanish.

8 years' experience managing facilities and support services.
Managed and developed **3 service departments** with a **staff of 40**. Reorganized and set quality standards to reduce costs and lower turnover. Implemented training programs, improved morale and the respect of workers for one another. Strong negotiation skills. Work with high technology applications. In a building of 50,000 sq. ft., responsible for **office planning, telecommunications, maintenance, and record retention.**

SUMMARY OF QUALIFICATIONS

Over 20 years' customer-service and operations experience with Uniroyal. Successful in managing and store operations. Also international business experience. Excellent communication and presentation skills. Speak Portuguese, Spanish and some Italian. Excellent computer skills (Uniroyal has one of the most modern computer systems). College degree. Establish a good rapport with clients of different socioeconomic levels.

20 years' experience in TV Production. Network and Local, Daytime and Primetime Dramatic Series. New York, Miami, Los Angeles. Intimate knowledge of scripts and work with writers. Strong production administration skills interfacing with and supervising crew, staff and budgets. Decision-maker responding to fast-paced quality production demands with a spirit of creative compatibility, stability, dedication and ease.

8 years' experience managing facilities and support services.
Managed and developed **3 service departments** with a **staff of 40**. Reorganized and set quality standards to reduce costs and lower turnover. Implemented training programs, improved morale and the respect of workers for each other. Strong negotiation skills. Work with high technology applications. In a building of 50,000 sq. ft., responsible for **office planning, telecommunications, maintenance, and record retention.**

A CPA/MBA with 14 years combined experience in finance, accounting and systems.
Seven years experience in the agricultural services industry.
An independent, goal-oriented problem solver with a record of success in
managing, organizing, streamlining and automating
administrative, operating and financial functions.

Twenty-five years with local, regional and national not-for-profit organizations
developing and administering self-supporting programs for members and the public.

Primary areas of interest:
- Designing programs and service-delivery systems
- Identifying and cultivating funding sources
- Recruiting and training volunteer leaders

---

11 years' experience in Juvenile Justice/Child Welfare Advocacy

- Managed staff of 60; 150 volunteers; 3 departments; budget of $2.2 million.
- Designed programs, facilities and information systems.
- Managed quality of service programs.

Set the tone for the quality of service provided by staff and volunteers.
Achieve organizational goals while maintaining excellent relationships.

Seven years' experience in all areas of kitchen management in a variety of established restaurants.

- Chez Marguerite • Saxony Hotel • Hyatt Hotel • The Square Plate

- Resourceful and organized manager; accepted additional responsibilities that easily fit into an already coordinated schedule.

  - Managed staff of 7
  - trained and developed staff
  - responsible for hiring
  - conscious of food costs
  - as a motivator and teacher, inspired staff to be reliable and organized

- Worked closely with owners and management to develop menu items that fit in with overall scheme. **Resulted in higher sales**.

- Can provide a **variety of cuisines and methods for preparation**:
  - various ethnic orientations: French, Italian, American, and so on
  - various levels of complexity; from simpler pasta dishes to foie gras and truffles

- Developed and implemented systems in all areas of kitchen:
  - operate **on schedule** regardless of interruptions or problems
  - quickly take over any area to keep production going
  - create a satisfying kitchen atmosphere
  - institute systems to maintain good sanitation habits

Degree, Culinary Institute of America
Eight years' business experience

Eight years as a <u>clinical nutrition specialist</u> in pediatrics and public health.
A solid background in basic <u>laboratory research</u>. Resourceful, persuasive, diplomatic, constructive and goal-oriented. Provide <u>consulting services to 15</u> non-profit, community and academic <u>institutions</u>. <u>Widely published</u> to lay and scientific audiences. Experience ranges from the care of individuals (infancy to middle-aged) to the planning of <u>national programs</u>. Have worked with all the major nutritional disorders. A specialist in the rehabilitation of failure-to-thrive children.

<u>6 years' international business/legal experience</u>. <u>Dual French and American citizenship</u>. Law degree. Have worked in Paris, New York, London. Also understand Italian, German, some Chinese. Strong interpersonal skills.

Summary of Qualifications

<u>General management executive</u>: <u>broadcasting, fund raising and promotion.</u>

- For over 20 years, <u>**owner/operator of two Mid-West radio stations**</u>.
  - Hosted two-hour <u>**radio talk show**</u> six days a week for 10 years.
- **A <u>seasoned idea-generator, fund raiser and promoter</u>.**
  - Motivate the general public to respond.
- **A <u>community leader</u>.**
  - <u>**Strong public image**</u> and inspire a high level of confidence.
  - Well-known and held in high regard.
  - Heavily involved in charitable and community needs.
- Resourceful, creative and ready to help.
  - <u>**Action-oriented, dynamic and persuasive.**</u>
  - Constant and loyal supporter.
- Degrees from Purdue and the University of Illinois (M.S.).

SUMMARY OF QUALIFICATIONS

18 years' proven project management experience
PC Computer systems, Training and Education, PC-Based business solutions
A PC problem-solver, developer and troubleshooter

- Designed, developed and managed state-of-the-art CBT programs that significantly enhance training experience and performance of participants.
- Managed the development of unique highly marketable real-time computerized simulation.
- 18 years of teaching, training and adult education.
- During two-year period, managed company's first PC Center devoted entirely to learning a fundamental new technology.
  - hired and managed instructor staff by matching needs of business unit to skills of instructors.
  - trained over 500 professionals of all levels in first year of operation.
  - taught classes in Lotus, WordPerfect, Dbase and DOS.
- Managed company's first-ever video conference for Chairman and President.

---

13 years' experience developing **corporate trademark promotions, special events and licensing campaigns**. Substantially increase revenues through the development of creative and unique concepts as well as detailed attention to follow-through. Extensive national, international and multi-national exposure. Interaction with CEO's of major corporations.

20 years' international business experience in:
- **international trade**   • **sales and marketing**   • **management**

Specialize in the Asia/Pacific region, especially Taiwan, Hong Kong and PC.

Strong <u>business negotiation skills with Asians</u>. <u>Established Asian subsidiaries</u> for three major U.S. corporations. <u>Strong company representative</u> for trade and operations both in Asia and the U.S. Speak nine Chinese dialects, English & Japanese. Bi-cultural. Outgoing and dedicated. Establish easy rapport with all levels of professional people. U.S. citizen.

18 years in <u>Corporate/Public Affairs</u> specializing in <u>international programs</u>

Work with top levels in corporate, government, international and philanthropic organizations. Routinely assigned sensitive and "impossible" major projects.

EXECUTIVE with 23 years of diversified experience in international and domestic markets. Includes ten years of P&L responsibility for businesses in Europe, Africa-Middle East, and Far East. Extensive experience in Latin and South America. Earlier experience in financial and manufacturing functions. Special skills in:

- Managing businesses to turn around performance and achieve full potential;
- Developing and implementing viable long-range plans, including marketing, product, operations, financial, and acquisition/divestiture strategies;
- Analyzing and controlling all aspects of business to reduce costs and improve profits;
- Organizing, training and motivating to improve individual and group effectiveness.

INTERNATIONAL HUMAN RESOURCES EXECUTIVE
Policy Development   Organizational Planning   Management Training

Over 15 years' experience in international human-resources environments. Solid capabilities in strategic planning, policy formulation, management development, succession planning, and recruitment.

Major accomplishments in improving productivity through executive development, management training, business development, and strategic planning. Additional skills in providing technical and professional assistance to start-ups in international markets.

Marketing Manager
specializing in major fund-raising/development/marketing activities/special events for not-for-profit agencies and small companies

Areas of Expertise
- Telemarketing • Broadcast Fund-raising • Direct Mail
- Media-Stimulated Calling • Major Special Events
- Membership/Customer/Constituency Development

- Created integrated campaigns including direct marketing, television, fund-raising, and so on.
- Managed telemarketing programs for organizations such as:
  - GTE • The United Way • UNICEF • Workforce America
- Conducted major television fund-raising campaigns.
- Managed all communications for the 1988 Democratic National Convention
  - Coordinated the work of 300 to 1000 people.

Seventeen years' experience in real estate: residential apartment acquisition and quality management, negotiating, banking relations, and contractor and tenant relations. Twenty years' experience in manufacturing including purchasing, inventory control, interpersonal relations, sales operations and quality management.

CONSUMER SALES AND MARKETING MANAGER

Areas of Expertise

- Sales Management
- Merchandising
- Telemarketing
- Brand Management
- Trade Shows/Sales Meetings
- Sales Incentive Programs
- Pricing, Packaging, Promotions
- Excellent Speaker

Managed staff of 12; $1.1 million budget. Took a brand with no exposure in the Michigan market: Grew it to $4 million within 3 months. Coordinated 2 key sales meetings and 2 retail trade shows.

Aggressive in the marketplace. Consistently a top performer.
Effectively organize and manage staff.

Hands-on Systems Manager
with strong technical competence in systems analysis and design, both batch and on-line.

- Routinely selected to manage the most critical, time-sensitive, and highly visible projects.
- Experienced in both batch and on-line in a wide variety of systems, such as:
  - Financial Systems
  - Network Systems
  - Order Processing/Quality Control
  - On-line Order Entry
- Insist on quality, resulting in a smooth implementation.
- Develop creative and innovative solutions that dramatically cut development time.
- Maintain strong relationships with all levels of users.
- Strong programming background: Assembler, COBOL, 4th Generation; Honeywell, IBM.
  - Learn on the job with little formal training.

INTERNATIONAL TELECOMMUNICATIONS EXECUTIVE

Eighteen years in <u>telecommunications</u>, twelve as <u>network manager/planner</u> for <u>large end-users</u>, six years in <u>market research</u> and forecasting. Experienced researcher in <u>radar techniques</u> including <u>antennas</u> and <u>signal processing</u>.

- Presented 3-year telecom plan to company executives.
- Upgraded company-wide voice/data network.
- Implemented Unicol's voice/data network.
- MBA, UCLA; MSEE, University of Michigan; BSEE, Georgia Institute of Technology

An innovative strategic marketer, manager, and research scientist with 10 years at IBM.

Launched new products in a highly competitive market. In-depth understanding of business, customers, competitors and the resulting products. Ph.D. in Chemistry; undergraduate in Pre-Med. Technical consultant to U.S. Navy. Six years in Research, Development and Manufacturing.

SUMMARY OF QUALIFICATIONS

Fifteen years' management experience with the State of California in
Data Processing, Telecommunications Networking, Computer Technology,
Data Center facilities-planning and construction.

- Managed a network of over 300 lines, over 3000 terminals, communicating with all major State buildings.
- Coordinated reconstruction of 10,000-sq.-ft. data center that met corporate standards.
- Planned security and implemented encryption for critical data communications lines.

Conduct timely implementation of new lines, new technology, equipment installation and follow-up.
Excellent rapport with other managers, end users, clients, and staff.

In the following résumé, the job hunter does not like his present job.
Therefore, in the summary he highlighted jobs he had six and ten years earlier:

Summary of Qualifications

Manager of Financial Planning and Analysis
with a public accounting background.

Industry Experience Includes:

- Retail   • Financial Services   • Transportation   • Communication   • Chemicals

For Macy's:
- wrote business plans for **store openings,**
- supervised and performed financial projections and **analysis of sites, competitors and demographics,**
- **coordinated five-year** and annual plans and quarterly and monthly budget,
- **wrote business plan** of a home-center chain.

In public accounting:
- selected to develop new audit techniques, which reduced costs of major audits,
- taught national and regional audit seminars.

MBA, Finance; BS, Finance and Accounting

SUMMARY OF QUALIFICATIONS

Accounting/operations executive with over 18 years of steadily increasing diverse management experience. Complex and sophisticated environments. Strong technical and analytical skills.

- Business experience ranges from securities and credit cards to travelers checks and mortgage servicing.
- Quantitative and analytical orientation - CPA.
- Managed both line operations and staff units from 5 professionals to over 50 people.
- Extensive user involvement in development of PC-based and mainframe-resident applications.
- Developed innovative strategies and methodologies to solve major problems.

PROFILE

Regional Sales Manager
Technology-based Industries

- **Staff of 20**.   • Revenue of $30 Million
- Consistently Exceeds Plan.
  - In three years at Wal-Mart, **doubled worldwide sales** of certain core products.
  - Obtained enthusiastic support from 16 internal organizations.
- In Houston during oil bust, managed major account sales group.
  - **Took it from last place to #2 in Xerox**.
  - Brought leadership, direction and focus to a disintegrating situation.
  - Achieved **11 President's Clubs**.
- Formally recognized for assembling **the most talented sales teams.**
- Strongly believe in results-centered management.

**Develop imaginative, profitable solutions consistently
delivered with the support of challenged, committed colleagues.**

SUMMARY OF QUALIFICATIONS

**A corporate trade finance and marketing executive
with 10 years' international and domestic experience.**

- Proven **generator of fee revenue** via financial advisory mandates.
- Structure and market cross-border trade finance solutions which **open foreign capital markets**.
- Experience in both the trading and financing of commodity trade flows.
- Identify, originate, structure and close **innovative and resourceful financial structures** for countries burdened with debt:

  - commodity/asset-based trade
  - debt swaps/liquidation
  - hedging techniques

  - commodity swaps
  - barter/countertrade/offset
  - unblocking of currencies

- Foreign sales management, product introduction and marketing experience

---

*CFO and General Manager.
Directed companies ranging from $100 million to over $1 billion.
Divisional as well as Corporate Management experience.*

Industry Specialties

- **Pharmaceuticals/Health Services**   • **Publishing**   • **International**
  - **Consumer Goods**   • **Manufacturing**

Chief Financial Officer
Specializing in turning around/growing medium-sized companies.

- A key member of the management team developing growth strategies while keeping the company under control.
- Set up the corporate structure for new subsidiaries.
- Rebuilt the financial organizations of two medium-sized companies, enabling them to raise significant capital.
- Attract and retain top quality people.

Areas of expertise:

- Finance
- Administration
- Real Estate
- Banking Relationships

Industry experience includes:

- Service Businesses
- Sports
- Construction
- Chemical/Manufacturing
- Perfume
- Retail

Business Manager
with strong customer-service management expertise.
Over 20 years in financial services and not-for-profit

- **Created** and directed **new business** opportunities and **turned around** performance.
  - As Business Manager, **increased profits 294%** over two years. Improved service 41%.
  - As Customer Service Consultant, measurably improved service in **60 locations**.
  - As Branch Manager, increased revenue 37% in one year; significantly improved service.
- As Board member for **three Not-for-Profit** organizations, directed programs that provided services to children, families, and people with AIDS.

Focus simultaneously on increasing revenue and improving service.
Noted for forming exceptionally strong relationships, motivating staff,
providing leadership, direction and spirit to get the job done.
Energetic, articulate, resourceful.

Chief Legal Executive
specializing in communications, information and entertainment.

A General Counsel:
manage internal lawyers; supervise outside counsel.

A deal-maker and senior legal advisor:
key member of the management team;
sophisticated in legal, financial and business dealings.

Human Resources Generalist

• **Financial Services**   • **Health Care**   • **Manufacturing**

Developed new programs/services. Achieved significant cost savings. Improved and enhanced existing services. Excellent presentation, negotiating and consulting skills. High standards of integrity, professionalism and teamplay. M.B.A.

Areas of Expertise

• Organizational Development	• Training and Development
• Employee Relations	• Agency Relationships
• Succession Planning	• Compensation
• Performance-based Management Systems	• Staffing and Mobility
• Employment Management	• Affirmative Action

Financial Services Technology Head
regularly selected to manage large, challenging development efforts.
Domestic and International

• Manage staffs of 150; budget of $25 - 30 million.

• Successful experience with large, "from scratch" development efforts:, both domestically and internationally. Responsible for:
    • management of all projects dealing with front-end systems **world-wide.**
    • development and maintenance of **all systems throughout Middle East and Africa.**
    • complete re-development of all product processing and administrative systems.

• **Saved $60 million** by renegotiating major purchasing agreements

A "hands-on" senior manager with very firm technical grounding.
Lead and motivate technical staffs while developing excellent user relationships.

SENIOR CORPORATE LEGAL MANAGER

for global organization with 100+ attorneys and annual profits of $1 billion.

GTE   DUPONT   NBC

Industry experience includes:

• consumer products	• information business
• media • communications/R&D	• chemicals, pharmaceuticals

• Senior legal advisor, **reporting directly to President and COO.**

• **Instituted and led** what culminated in a **judicial victory for entire industry.**

• **Successfully prosecuted copyright-infringement suit against major competitor**.
    • Achieved strategic goal of maintaining customers and revenues.

Recognized for reflective and open analytical methods,
astute business-counseling skills and ability to provide strategic focus
with respect to company's domestic and international consumer businesses.

Project Manager specializing in service businesses

- Managed projects of up to 120 people; budgets of up to $30 million; both domestically and internationally.

- Expert in the use of project-management software tools and techniques.

- Built diverse applications on multiple software and hardware platforms.

  - Built and implemented $20-million **integrated customer information system.** Hired and trained highly skilled project team.

  - Developed and installed a **generic package** that satisfied the needs of companies in <u>28 countries</u>.

  - Managed relaunching of proprietary <u>credit card</u>. Total responsibility for all specifications, hardware, code development and implementation.

  - Experience as both a line and matrix manager.

  - CASE-tool experienced.

Start projects from scratch, build strong project plans and strong loyal teams. Known for being able to resolve "impossible" problems and motivate demoralized staff.

Audit Executive - Multinational Environment

Involved in auditing all aspects of the Corporation including Technology. Managed Multicurrency Audit Budgets up to $20 million. 14 years' experience in interfacing with Audit Committees, Secretary since 1981.

- **Managed multinational, multilingual global audit staffs - up to 340 people.**
  - **Able to deal with any audit issue.**
  - **Resources, expertise and technical skills were shared globally.**
  - **Put in streamlined audit processes and automated audit systems.**
- **Have reported directly to Chief Auditor or CEO continuously since 1974.**
- **Developed Audit Strategic Plan focusing on Business and Audit Risk.**
  - **Encouraged auditors to take prudent risks.**
- **Substantially improved reward systems and visibility for the Audit staff.**
- **Regularly address audiences of up to 200 people on Auditing Topics.**
- **MBA, CPA, and Chartered Auditor.**

Senior Sales
and Client Management Executive

with a track record of creating substantial new business income.

*Manage the start-up, turn-around, and enhancement
of corporate finance relationships and lines of business.*

- **AMBRACK** • **HAGEN-ROGERS** • **WILDE-LORD**

- A generalist, with a current specialization in **Telecommunications, Publishing and Information companies**.

- Significant domestic and international market experience:
  - in corporate, not-for-profit, and government agency client markets,
  - in both wholesale and retail.

- Management experience in both short- and long-range planning, corporate development, risk management, project management, and building new lines-of-business.

GENERAL COUNSEL
**with a staff of 40 lawyers
specializing in health law, environmental law and public policy**

- Key member of management team of 2000-person organization with $500 million budget.

- Intimate knowledge of **important State and Federal government agencies** responsible for Health, Insurance, Social Services, and Environmental Conservation.

- **Negotiated a dozen landmark health laws of national significance,** major consent agreements, and intra- and inter-agency agreements.

- Organized, led and reported on **major investigations of government corruption** and mismanagement. Resulted in major legislation, dismissals, and program improvements.

- Serve as public spokesperson for State Department of Health on key health issues including medical malpractice, government reorganization, regulatory reform.

*Excellent judgment, high integrity.
Able to organize and motivate large groups.*

IV.

DEVELOPING
YOUR RÉSUMÉ

The dynamic principle of fantasy is play, which belongs also to the child, and . . . appears to be inconsistent with the principle of serious work. But without this playing with fantasy, no creative work has ever yet come to birth.

Carl Jung

. . . my experience says that it is possible to study and imagine where we may be headed. By imagining where we are going, we reduce this complexity, this unpredictability which. . . encroaches upon our lives.

Peter Schwartz,
The Art of the Long View

The Typical Résumé: Historical

Most résumés are historical documents. They list the positions a person has had and what the person did in each position. It's as if the résumé writer were saying: "I've put it all down. Now you figure out where I fit in or what I should be doing next."

But if the reader doesn't "get it"-- doesn't figure out what you could do for him or her—you will be passed over.

A good résumé allows readers to imagine you working in their company. Something in the résumé grabs them, and they can see some as-yet-undefined possibility for you.

Your Résumé: Strategic

Your résumé should not be a historical document, but a future-oriented, strategic one. It should select from your background and highlight those areas you want to offer and state them in ways that relate to the needs of the market.

- What kinds of things would you like to do next?
- What do you have to offer that the market may also want?
- And what do you have to offer that may give you credibility or negotiating leverage (as in "I'll do this for you, providing you allow me to do this other thing.")?

Use the Language of Your Target Market

Restate your background in terms your target market will understand. Do not use the lingo of your present industry or company. For example, if you want to switch from education to a training position in the corporate world, remember that corporate life does not have "teachers." It has "trainers" or even "instructors." Consider using these words instead. Do not expect employers to translate the terminology. Make it easy for them to see how you fit in and let

them see that you understand their business.

If you have worked for a major corporation, do not use the company jargon.

Think about how you want to "position" yourself to the reader.

The Purpose of Your Résumé

Your résumé serves a number of purposes:

1. It is your marketing piece.

To test your résumé, scan it and see what story comes across during the first 10 seconds. The length of your résumé does not matter. We don't care whether or not they even read your résumé. What we care about is whether or not they call you in for an interview.

At this point, you are not looking for a job—you are looking for an interview—an opportunity to explore.

The scenario is something like this: Your résumé and cover letter cross the desk of someone in a position to hire you or recommend that you be hired. Something in these documents catches the reader's imagination. They have no official job openings, but . . . Oh well, why not call you in just to chat?

At this point, you are not looking for a job—you are looking for an interview—a meeting to have the opportunity to explore what is going on in their company and tell them more about you. You want to build a relationship and see if perhaps there is a place for you *in the long run*.

2. It is your sales tool in your absence.

After you leave the meeting, the manager may want to discuss you with someone else. Your résumé can speak for you in your absence and convince the other person that you have a lot to offer.

3. It can guide your interview.

You have complete control over what the reader sees. If you highlight certain areas, the reader can't help but ask about them. If you play down or even leave out certain things, you reduce the chances of having the interview center on those areas.

We each have things we'd like to talk about and things we'd rather not. Emphasize those parts of your background that are:

- things you have done well and also enjoyed doing and would like to do again;
- areas that make you more marketable by differentiating you from your likely competitors;
- areas that support your "pitch"—the main argument you are advancing about yourself;
- things you think will "sell" you and will be of interest to the readers in your marketplace.

General Guidelines for Writing Résumés

1. Before you start, do yourself a favor. Go back and do the Seven Stories Exercise. The effort you put into this will dramatically affect the quality of your résumé. It will give you the substance you need to work with, and add depth and detail to your résumé in those areas you want to highlight. It will also loosen you up and increase your chances of telling a good story about yourself.

Whether I'm working with someone making $20,000 a year or $400,000, they each go through this exercise. Then I have a better idea of what they may want to emphasize on their résumés, and what they'd rather not highlight. If your past accomplishments are important to you, they should take up some room on your résumé.

2. Most people need only one résumé. However, this book does present a person with two résumés.

3. Aim to have a reverse chronological résumé (starting with your most recent job). Functional résumés are organized by type of work done rather than by dates. They are usually written to hide something, and they are looked upon with suspicion. Chances are, there is a way for you to say what you want to say without resorting to a totally functional résumé. For example, try a chronological résumé that has a particular job broken down functionally.

4. You generally do not need an objective statement. Objectives *limit* your search. Sometimes an objective is appropriate, such as in the case where the job hunter wants to reassure the hiring manager that he truly is interested in the area he is looking at.

5. **Always have a summary statement on your résumé**. It's an opportunity to dramatically influence the way the reader sees you and the rest of the information you have included. Take advantage of this powerful tool. But remember, it's not easy. (The cover letter is your other opportunity for positioning what the reader notices in your résumé.)

If your résumé positions you the way you want to be positioned, it's a good résumé. If it doesn't, it's not good.

Is This Résumé Good or Bad?

Now take a look at the sample résumés. You'll see that it is difficult to judge whether a résumé is good or bad unless you know the circumstances and the pitch the person is trying to make.

People show me résumés all the time and ask me to quickly tell them if

the résumés are good or bad. Usually, the ones that have no summary statement are not very good. And those written with lots of large paragraphs are difficult to read (the messages get lost in the middle of those paragraphs). But other than that, I frankly cannot tell if a résumé is good or bad. I need to know more about the person and his or her goals. If your résumé positions you the way you want to be positioned, it's a good résumé. If it doesn't, it's not good.

Unlike other résumé books, this one is geared to showing you the reasoning behind the résumé.

I hope the following case studies will show you the power of a correctly positioned résumé--one that places you at the proper level and highlights the right areas from your background.

My clients have been delighted with the difference a good résumé can make in their searches. And I am delighted to pass on some of this wisdom to you.

Many of life's failures are people who did not realize how close they were to success when they gave up.
Thomas Edison

Perseverance is a great element of success. If you only knock long enough and loud enough at the gate, you are sure to wake up somebody.
Longfellow

A life requires thorough preparation. We must rid ourselves of the idea that there's a short-cut to achievement.
George Washington Carver, former slave who transformed the pattern of agriculture throughout the South

---

I never hit a shot, not even in practice, without having a very sharp, in-focus picture of it in my head.
Jack Nicklaus, as quoted by Jack Maguire, *Care and Feeding of the Brain*

Résumé Length

In the old days, just a few years ago, résumés were one page long. Most people had worked at the same company--and often the same job--for most of their careers. They were expected to stay put. Their entire history could usually fit on one page.

Those who changed jobs were often limited to doing again what they had done before. What's more, they were competing in an unsophisticated market. Job hunters were not trained to beat out their competition.

Things have changed dramatically in the past few years. Today, the average American has been in his or her job only four years, and the average person getting out of college today can expect to have twelve to fifteen jobs in a lifetime. Simply listing all the jobs one has had could easily take a page--without mentioning what a person has done in those jobs.

Furthermore, the job-hunting market has become more sophisticated. It is more important to not be "rejected on paper." This means that you have something on your résumé that causes them not to want to meet you. With our more complex work experiences, it is important to position ourselves to fit into the various markets we may be targeting. While you want your résumé to be as brief as possible and still get your message across, it may end up being more than one page long. And that's not necessarily a negative.

Dates on Right

Job hunters used to put the dates of employment down the left side of the résumé. But now, with people having so many jobs, there might be a string of dates down the left-hand side of the résumé. Since the reader's eye naturally goes to the left column, the dates become the main message. That's why the trend these days is to put dates on the right.

First, Decide the Story You Want To Tell

Form follows function. Decide the story you want to tell a specific target market, and tell it as briefly as is sensible. Then decide what format to use.

Do What is Appropriate for Your Level

In the examples on the following pages, a very senior executive may have a one-, two-, three-, or four-page résumé. It depends on how complicated the person's message is.

However, a junior person should never have a three- or four-page résumé. It is inappropriate, and makes the person look silly. One page--or two at most--is appropriate.

Middle managers almost always require two pages, and sometimes three, to tell their stories in a way that is clear.

Think about what will show up on your first page. Your summary is most important. If the jobs you want the reader to see are also on the first page, that's lucky. But if the jobs you want the reader to see are on your second page, you will wind up with a longer summary because you will have to include in the summary information about those jobs that appear later.

This can happen when the situation you are in right now does not lend itself to where you want to go next. In that case, format your résumé so the reader's eye will see your summary, skip over your most recent job, and then go directly to the one before that. Simply boldface or underline phrases in your summary and in the body of the résumé to highlight the job you want to call attention to.

Scan your résumé to see where your eye naturally goes. That is the message your reader will get too.

V.

RÉSUMÉ
CASE STUDIES

Tom Warren:
What Did He <u>Really</u> Do?

We are challenged on every hand to work untiringly to achieve excellence in our lifework. Not all men are called to specialized or professional jobs; even fewer rise to the heights of genius in the arts and sciences; many are called to be laborers in factories, fields, and streets. But no work is insignificant. All labor that uplifts humanity has dignity and importance and should be undertaken with painstaking excellence. If a man is called to be a street sweeper, he should sweep streets even as Michelangelo painted, or Beethoven composed music, or Shakespeare wrote poetry. He should sweep streets so well that all the host of heaven and earth will pause to say, "Here lives a great street sweeper who did his job well."

Martin Luther King, Jr.

Tom Warren's old résumé is pretty standard: he states the jobs he's had and what he did in each one. It's the same old historical approach.

The problem is that his résumé leaves out all of the important parts. For his new résumé, we simply added four parts: the all-important summary and three introductory paragraphs that state what Tom *really* did in each job. (For the purposes of this example, we have reproduced only the first page of Tom's two-page résumé.)

For example, in the last job on the page, he states that he managed eight Manhattan branches. We had already completed his Seven Stories Exercise, so I knew there was more to his personality than this implied. Here is how our discussion went:

Kate: "Tom, do you want to manage bank branches?"
Tom: "Not a chance. I hate branch management."
Kate: "But this résumé positions you, among other things, as a branch manager."
Tom: "That's what I did in that job."
Kate (I try to provoke him): "But to me this sounds so boring. What did you really do in that job? What is it you brag to your wife that you did?"
Tom: "Kate, you don't understand. That job was important. *I turned around the largest problem-ridden branch business in the company.*"
Kate: "Oh, excuse me, Tom. How could I have known? I don't see that on your résumé. Let's put it on there. Now, what kinds of things would you like to do next?"
Tom: "I want to build major businesses or turn around problem brands."
Kate: "Have you done those things before?"
Tom: "Yes, I definitely have."

Kate: "Then let's put that in your summary. It will dramatically increase your chances of getting to do those things again. "

That's what you have to do too. For most people, the problem is not that they stretch the truth on their résumés; the problem is that they don't say what they *really* did.

Figuring this out is much more difficult than simply reciting your job description. That's why it's important to do the Seven Stories Exercise (which you will find in the front of this book and in *Through the Brick Wall*). The exercise helps you step back from a résumé frame-of-mind so you can concentrate on the most important accomplishments of your life. Then the exercise helps you to think about each accomplishment: what led up to it, what your role was, what gave you satisfaction, what your motivation was, and so on.

We added those parts to Tom's résumé and left the rest alone. In fact, the parts we added are the only parts that really matter—so those are highlighted and the rest becomes the background. Now Tom has a good sales piece—one that truly reflects what he did.

This new résumé is a strategic document. It looks ahead, not back. It thinks about what he would like to do next, and then finds those experiences in his background that support what he wants to do. In addition, it highlights those areas that were the most satisfying. Now he has increased his chances of finding a new job where he repeats or builds on those satisfying experiences.

THOMAS WARREN

2343 Fifth Avenue
New York, New York 11000

Home: 212-333-4444
Business: 212-555-1111

PREMIERBANK   1983-Present

International Institutions Group   1992-Present
Director of Electronic Banking

Responsible for support and development of all interbank payment and information systems.

* Developed and market tested a new offline funds transfer product.
* Upgraded and repositioned existing worldwide online payment system.
* Created line-wide repricing plan to maximize target customer penetration.
* Developed strategy to integrate payment, information and securities products.

New York Retail Bank   1990-1991
Director, Special Marketing Group

Responsible for growth and profitability of the New York Bank's $13-Billion consumer portfolio. Managed new product development, pricing and sales promotion.

* Developed, positioned and introduced the PremierBank Investment Portfolio, PremierBank's first mass-market integrated investment product. Created new portfolio-selling concept to incorporate it into the branch sales process.
* Established more efficient PremierBank core-account promotion tactics.
* Developed new investment savings product.
* Created unique research method to guide new product development.

Senior Area Director, Financial District   1990

Managed eight Manhattan branches with $31-million net revenue and $1.2-billion total footings. Responsible for total branch performance including sales, service, control, revenue and expenses.

* Put new management team in place in three key branches.
* Reversed balance declines by revitalizing business-account marketing.
* Established distribution strategy and plan for World Trade Center marketplace, including customer and business offsites.
* Developed a high-net-worth tailored credit program for area with $2 million-$3 million annual revenue potential.
* Initiated regional staffing efficiency analysis, which significantly improved branch productivity.

THOMAS WARREN

2343 Fifth Avenue
New York, New York 11000

Home: 212-333-4444
Business: 212-555-1111

SUMMARY

Innovative financial-services marketer with ten years at PremierBank and heavy package-goods product-management experience. Created new products. Built major businesses. Turned around problem brands. Strong strategic thinker and team builder.

Areas of Expertise

o **Product Management**	o **Electronic Banking**
o **New Product Development**	o **Branch Banking**
o **Sales Management**	o **Market Analysis**

PREMIERBANK   1983-Present

International Institutions Group   1992-Present
Director of Electronic Banking

Created a multi-year business plan to restore PremierBank's leadership in interbank electronic payments through the worldwide rollout of superior offline payment products.

Responsible for support and development of all interbank payment and information systems.
* Developed and market tested a new offline funds-transfer product.
* Upgraded and repositioned existing worldwide online payment system.
* Created line-wide repricing plan to maximize target customer penetration.
* Developed strategy to integrate payment, information and securities products.

New York Retail Bank   1990-1991
Director, Special Marketing Group

Created the New York retail bank's first effective way to package and sell its diverse investment product line.

Responsible for growth and profitability of the New York Bank's $13-billion consumer portfolio. Managed new product development, pricing and sales promotion.
* Developed, positioned and introduced the PremierBank Investment Portfolio, PremierBank's first mass-market integrated investment product. Created new portfolio selling concept to incorporate it into the branch sales process.
* Established more efficient PremierBank core-account promotion tactics.
* Developed new investment-savings product.
* Created unique research method to guide new product development.

Senior Area Director, Financial District   1990

Reorganized and redirected a large, problem-ridden branch business to restore balance and revenue growth.

Managed eight Manhattan branches with $31-million net revenue and $1.2-billion total footings. Responsible for total branch performance including sales, service, control, revenue and expenses.

The approach Wally used in his résumé used to be okay for someone just getting out of school: he stated a career objective, which was followed by his education and then a historical listing of his work experience. Today we live in an age of sound bites and résumé overload. It would have taken the reader too long to figure out what level Wally was at, the important things he had done, and where he might fit in.

Wally's "after" résumé has a summary, which makes it easy for the reader to figure out exactly what he does, and his level. In addition, the reader gets a feel for Wally's personality: "an innovator with people, processes, and equipment." Wally's old résumé told us nothing about his work style.

Wally had one more problem: the large number of jobs he had held. On the "before" résumé, the dates down the left certainly highlighted his job changes.

A number of those job changes were easily explained, but Wally didn't get the chance to explain them because prospective employers formed their own opinions. Wally was "rejected on paper." He had written something a prospective employer might object to. Do not allow your résumé to defeat you. Handle those objections "on paper."

In this case, Wally inserted--in small type--the reasons he left a number of those jobs: the company moved, closed, or other explanations that do not reflect on Wally at all. The explanation is not included for every job--just enough to let the reader know that Wally would and could have stayed longer if the circumstances had been right.

With so many companies in trouble these days, a job hunter may change jobs through no fault of his or her own. It *may* be best to let the reader know those reasons--on paper. But don't overdo it and feel compelled to put in a reason for every job you've left.

Finally, the résumé is scannable. It is now two pages long, but the reader is more likely to notice the things Wally thinks are important.

WALLACE M. PETERSEN
20 Midwood Road
Strathmore, New Jersey 05555
Telephone: 609-555-3412

Height: 5'10"
Weight: 185 lbs.
Birth date: Dec. 22, 1954
Married - 3 children

CAREER OBJECTIVE:	To gain a position with a firm that offers a challenging opportunity which utilizes a background of actual press work combined with supervisory responsibilities and an opportunity for advancement.
EDUCATION:	CAMDEN COLLEGE, Blackwood, NJ Associate Degree in Business Administration Major: Business Management; Elective: Two years of Spanish
EXPERIENCE: Dec. 1989 to present	BUCKMASTER ASSOCIATES, Ivytown, PA Responsible for creating a web-printing operation, which involved traveling the country to locate, negotiate, purchase, erect and manage the operation, which consisted of two web presses, one sheet-fed press and a prep room, which included an Opti-copy Camera-Imposer. Other duties included negotiating with vendors for best supplies and prices and building a competent work force which stressed high production <u>and</u> quality with low operating cost. Very successful and efficient.
Oct. 1982 to Dec. 1989	PONTIAC PRESS, INC., Philadelphia BERTRAM COMMUNICATIONS, INC., subsidiary Hired initally to operate Pontiac's 4 unit, 2 folder Harris Press. After demonstrating the ability to motivate press crews and substantially increase production in a union environment, appointed to direct and manage the press-room operations of a new experimental plant. It is widely known to have been an outstanding success.
Dec. 1981 to Oct. 1982	A.D. WEINSTEIN LITHOGRAPH Hollywood, FL Pressman with extensive Heatset background on Harris M-1000, M-200, ATF, and Hantscho, all with double four-color (8 units) Butler and Wood Splicers, Tec and Offen Dryers, Combination and Double Former Folders, Sheeters, and one Ribbon Folder.
May 1976 to Dec. 1981	MACMILLAN PUBLISHING COMPANY Hired as Pressman's Helper. Promoted to lead 4-color Pressman. After 3 years, promoted to Working Supervisor. Experience on Harris 845 with 4 units, Harris V-25 with 7 units, 4 butlers, 4 pass dryer, chill tower, combination folder, three knife trimmers, Martin Tensimatic unit, in-line glueing system. Four-color process work on publication and news-paper supplements. Experienced on coated offset, and newsprint paper.
June 1974 to May 1976	ACME PRINTING COMPANY Hired as Flyboy of Goss Community Five-unit press. Promoted to Asst. Pressman.

Wallace M. Petersen

20 Midwood Road
Strathmore, New Jersey 05555
Residence: 609-555-3412

Summary of Qualifications

Web Press Supervisor/Manager
with 20 years' experience
and an emphasis on quality and productivity.

- **A hands-on supervisor**. Inspire workers to take pride in quality/quantity of their work.
  - Train workers to become independent, high-quality producers.
  - Select/retain the best people: self-starters with an eye on quality and productivity.
- An innovator with people, processes, and equipment:
  - Regularly develop **time-saving and cost-saving methods**.
- A **strong negotiator**: for both equipment and supplies. Resulted in substantial savings.
- Proficient in **rebuilding equipment**. Reduced machine downtime and costs.

Professional Experience

Web Operations Manager

1989-present

Buckmaster Associates **(specialized exclusively in printing jobs for other printers)**

Set up and managed a web-press operation. Company formerly had none.

- **Built a competent work-force:** stressed high production *and* quality with low operating cost.
  - As **printers for the trade**, our customers demanded the highest quality at a price where they could still make a profit reselling our work.
- Built from the ground up a cost-effective, highly productive web-printing operation.
  - Engineered the entire setup, determined the equipment needs, and negotiated the purchase of used equipment.
  - Hired/managed daily operations of this **20-person shop** with two 36" web presses, one sheet-fed press, and a prep room.
- Researched nationally to locate, select, negotiate, and purchase equipment.
  - Oversaw the reconditioning/rebuilding/assembling of 7 printing units, 2 folders, 5 splicers, and 2 counter-stackers. Made it operational **within 2 months**.
  - **Saved the company $300,000** versus the price of already refurbished equipment.
  - To produce the highest-quality work, personally supervised the erection of two 36" web presses and one sheet-fed press to **tolerances of 1/1000^{ths} of an inch**.
- Designed the prep room for good work flow (**Opti-copy Camera-Imposer**, plate burners, light tables, plate processors). **Saved $200,000**.
- Negotiated with vendors for prices usually given only to very large companies.
  - **Saved $500,000** per year.

Web Manager/Working Supervisor   1982-1989

Bertram Communications, Inc., subsidiary of **Pontiac Press, Inc.**

Set up and managed web operation, as working supervisor.

- **Payback on investment accomplished in only 14 months.**
- Developed a highly-motivated workforce.
    - The plant regularly attracted visitors who wanted to observe the operation.
    - The cleanliness of the workplace inspired pride in the workers.
- Produced **high-quality** work. Work formerly done on sheet-fed presses because of quality requirements was done on web at a tremendous cost savings.
- Developed **innovative** press folder **techniques** and conversions.

Reason for leaving: Entire plant moved to New York.

Pressman, A.D. Weinstein Lithograph   1981-1982

- Extensive Heat-set background on Harris M-1000, M-200, ATF, and Hantscho, all with double four-color (8 units) Butler and Wood Splicers, Tec and Offen Dryers. Combination and Double Former Folders, Sheeters, and one Ribbon Folder.

- A.D. Weinstein is almost exclusively a publication printer producing products such as *Time magazine*, *Cosmopolitan*, *Good Housekeeping*, *Eastern Review*, etc.

Reason for leaving: When mail rates went up, company could no longer compete.

Working Supervisor, Macmillan Publishing Company   1976-1981

Hired as Pressman's Helper. **Promoted to lead 4-color Pressman at age 23.**
After 3 years, promoted to Working Supervisor.

Experience on Harris 845 with 4 units, Harris V-25 with 7 units, 4 butlers, 4 pass dryer and chill tower, combination folder, three knife trimmers, Martin Tensimatic unit, in-line glueing system. Four-color process work on publication and newspaper supplements. Experienced on coated offset, and newsprint paper.

Assistant Pressman, Acme Printing Company   1974-1976

Hired as Flyboy of Goss Community five-unit press. Promoted to Asst. Pressman.

EDUCATION

Associate Degree in Business Administration, Camden College, 1975
Major: Business Management; Elective: Two years of Spanish

Julia Harris: Overcoming an Objection on Paper

You gain strength, courage and confidence by every experience in which you really stop to look fear in the face. You are able to say to yourself, "I lived through this horror. I can take the next thing that comes along." . . . You must do the thing you think you cannot do.
Eleanor Roosevelt, *You Learn by Living*

Peak performers have one leading trait: a sense of mission. A study of over 1,500 peak performers found that their single most commonly shared trait was the possession of a goal they were passionate about and were committed to achieving. They combined hard work with their other competitive traits (which varied) to accomplish the goal. Top performance was the result. Key: With a goal you believe in, hard work makes sense.
Dr. Charles Garfield, *Personnel Journal*, as quoted in *Boardroom Reports*, September 1, 1991

We often injure our cause by calling in that which is weak to support that which is strong.
Charles Caleb Colton

Julia had spent some time as an actor. When hiring managers saw this, it became an objection on paper, and they didn't want to see her. It overshadowed the solid corporate experience she already had. What's more, if she did get in for an interview, managers probed to find out why she had chosen acting as a career. It made her business experience look less substantial.

On her revised résumé, a summary statement puts a corporate spin on her theater experience (which included more than acting), and highlights her education more.

In addition, she dropped the name of the second company on her résumé (Golden Bo Tree East Co.), since it is irrelevant and distracting.

When testing your résumé in the market, notice if anything about your background is operating as a handicap for you. Think of how you can reposition this part to downplay it and how you can highlight those parts you want the reader to focus on.

JULIA G. HARRIS

355 South York Avenue
New York, New York 10483

Home: (212) 555-2351
Office: (212) 555-3320

EXPERIENCE

Amrock, New York
1988 - Present

Management Development Associate. In-house Corporate Human Resources consultant. Developed, designed and implemented vehicles to enhance Human Resource professionalism within Amrock world-wide. Accomplishments include:

- Executive Development - Created and implemented nomination process whereby top performers are selected to attend Executive Education programs. Coordinated the entire process, serving as a liaison between the university and participants to ensure appropriate developmental match.

- High Potential Development - Initiated database to: identify and source candidates for potential job assignments; track institutional progress; follow up on development plans.

- Focus Groups - Assessment of Development Needs - Managed all aspects of project design and implementation: met with senior management; prepared protocol; conducted sessions with over 120 HR professionals both in the U.S. and Europe; analyzed and integrated data.

- Questionnaire Development - Designed feedback instrument for HR professionals worldwide to elicit recommendations on key HR development needs.

- Program Development - Researched and designed seminars for senior human resources offsite. Included compensation seminars on Incentive Plan Design, Long Term Incentive and Tax Effective Comp. Coached presenters through feedback sessions.

Golden Bo Tree East Co., Ltd., Bangkok, Thailand
1987

Organization Development Consultant. Process consultant to senior management on cross-cultural issues around goal clarification, decision making, and team building. Resulted in improved organizational effectiveness in adapting to Thailand business demands.

Actor
1979 - 1985

EDUCATION

Columbia University, New York, New York; **Master of Arts**-Organizational Psychology   1987 - 1988
Awarded Academic Scholarship-**3.7 G.P.A.**

New York University, New York, New York; **Master of Arts**-Counseling Psychology   1985 - 1987
Awarded Academic Scholarship-**3.6 G.P.A.**

Utah State University, Bachelor of Fine Arts-Acting   1975 - 1979
        Awarded Full Tuition Scholarship

PUBLICATIONS

A Case Study: Organization Development in a Health Care System
New York University Psychology Quarterly - September, 1987

ADDITIONAL INFORMATION

Languages: Thai
Affiliations: American Psychological Association; NY Organization Development Network
Computer Skills: Macintosh II, Software - Microsoft Word 3.0; Q&A; SPSSX

JULIA G. HARRIS

355 South York Avenue
New York, New York 10483

Home: (212) 555-2351
Office: (212) 555-3320

Management/Organization Development Specialist

**Over 8 years of development and stand-up experience.
Financial, Entertainment and Exporting Industries.**

- Proven consulting expertise in:
- Executive and High Potential Development
- Needs Assessment
- Organizational Research
- Two master's degrees in Organizational and Counseling Psychology.
- Extensive exposure in Southeast Asia; Fluent in Thai.

Professional Experience

Amrock, New York   1988 - Present

Manager of Management Development

In-house Corporate Human Resources consultant. Developed, designed and implemented vehicles to enhance the professionalism of over 2,000 officers worldwide.

Accomplishments include:

- **High-Potential Development**
  Assess and identify top performers to: meet specific business talent needs; attend Executive University programs; facilitate succession planning.

- **Executive Development**
  Created and implemented nomination process whereby top performers are selected to attend Executive Education programs. Coordinated the entire process, serving as a liaison between the university and participants to ensure appropriate developmental match.

- **Focus Groups - Assessment of Development Needs**
  Managed all aspects of project design and implementation: met with senior management; prepared protocol; conducted sessions with over 500 officers throughout the U.S. and Europe; analyzed and integrated data.

- **Organizational Research**
  Use of statistical and research design (SPSSX) to conduct surveys, climate studies, turnover studies. Designed feedback instrument for HR professionals worldwide to elicit recommendations on key training needs.

- **Program Development**
  Researched and designed seminars for senior offsite. Included compensation seminars on Incentive Plan Design, Long Term Incentive and Tax Effective Comp. Coached presenters through feedback sessions.

Organization Development Consultant, Bangkok,Thailand   1987

For a major exporting company.

- Process consultant to senior management on cross-cultural issues.
- Impacted company structure, decision making, and team building.
- Resulted in improved organizational effectiveness in adapting to Thailand business demands.

The Shubert Organization, New York   1979 - 1985

- Read and edited scripts to determine commercial marketability.
- Developed and made presentations to prestigious audiences.

EDUCATION

Columbia University; **Master of Arts**-Organizational Psychology, 1987 - 1988
Awarded Academic Scholarship-**3.7 G.P.A**.

New York University; **Master of Arts**-Counseling Psychology, 1985 - 1987
Awarded Academic Scholarship-**3.6 G.P.A.**

Utah State University; **Bachelor of Fine Arts**-Acting, 1975 - 1979
Awarded Full Tuition Scholarship

PUBLICATIONS

A Case Study: Organization Development in a Health Care System
New York University Psychology Quarterly - September, 1987

ADDITIONAL INFORMATION

Languages: Thai
Affiliations: American Psychological Association; METRO; New York OD Network
Computer Skills: Macintosh II, Software - Microsoft Word 3.0; Q&A; SPSSX

David Walters:Handled His Fear of Discrimination

No spring nor summer beauty hath such grace,
As I have seen in one autumnal face.
John Donne, *The Autumnal*

At thirty, man suspects himself a fool;
Knows it at forty, and reforms his plan.
Edward Young

If man is to vanish from the earth, let him vanish in the moment of creation, when he is creating something new, opening a path to the tomorrow he may never see. It is man's nature to reach out, to grasp for the tangible on the way to the intangible.
Louis L'Amour, *The Lonesome Gods*

(The secret of how) to live without resentment or embarrassment in a world in which I was different from everyone else . . . . was to be indifferent to that difference.
Al Capp, "My Well-Balanced Life on a Wooden Leg," *Life*, May 23, 1960

David was worried that he would have difficulty finding a new position because he was an older man and lacked formal schooling. Yet, using the following résumé, he received four excellent offers within a very short time.

David has steadily advanced in his career. To those within his industry, every line on his résumé is impressive. In his summary, David notes how he is different from others in his field.

The résumé is compact and clear--eliminating any accomplishment that would be considered routine.

No one even noticed that David had not gone to college. What's more, no one could have accomplished what David had without having been around a few years. His age actually became an advantage.

Most job hunters have something that they think will keep them from getting their next job. It could be that they feel they are too young or too old, have too little education or too much, are of the wrong race, creed, nationality, sex or sexual orientation, weight or height, or are very aware that they have a physical disability.

While it is true that there is prejudice out there, job hunters who are too self-conscious about their perceived handicaps will hold themselves back.

In addition, they may inadvertently draw attention to their "problem" during the interview. Your attitude must be: "What problem? There is no problem. Let me tell you about the things I've done."

DAVID WALTERS

942 Cherry Hill Road
Los Angeles, CA 99125

Business: 222 555-3907
Home: 222 555-1074

SUMMARY OF QUALIFICATIONS

Treasury executive with over 20 years of international as well as domestic experience. Possess a clear understanding of the basic interrelationship of all aspects of the financial markets. At the forefront of simple, innovative solutions that are easily acceptable to others and later adopted at large. Record of generating new customer business. Lived and worked in many countries. Proficient in a number of languages. Strong turn-around and people-management skills.

EXPERIENCE

AMBANK, N.A.   **1966 - Present**

Individual Bank   1986 - Present
Vice President/Regional Treasurer
Middle East/Africa & Greece - Dubai

Established and controlled Treasury Units for the Individual Bank in Greece, Saudi Arabia, Oman, Bahrain and the U.A.E. to manage the risks of a portfolio totaling $3,200 billion.

- Set up Treasury function in 3 countries. Earned $2 million in 1988 ($1 million above budget).
- Developed a unique funding strategy that overcame local regulatory restrictions and reduced Ambank (Greece) borrowing costs by 5%.
- Developed a hedging strategy in highly restricted market. Avoided losses in excess of $1 million.
- Analyzed and identified the liquidity and interest-rate risks inherent in the business and developed and implemented a strategic plan to manage the risk.
- More than doubled foreign-exchange business in one year.

Investment Bank   1985 - 1986
Vice President/Treasurer - Panama

Created and managed a team of 7 professionals to control funding and liquidity of $350 million, managed Foreign Exchange, and observed regulatory constraints.

- Reorganized the treasury to address foreign-exchange needs. Expanded the marketing function.
- Increased corporate FX business tenfold in 14 months. Expanded FX into Central American currencies (Ambank became a "Market Maker" in Central American currencies).
- Installed an independent system to record Ambank's liquidity position in order to implement effective funding and reduce risk.
- Structured and implemented one of the first 3rd-party debt deals in Central America. Reduced El Salvador's debt at substantial savings. Ambank's first year intermediary fee exceeded $100 million.

Institutional Bank   1981 - 1985
<u>**Vice President/Training Center Administration Manager**</u> - **Puerto Rico**

Brought in to design and teach courses to develop Treasury in Latin America. Managed a team who coordinated all training-center courses.

- Developed treasury courses for all management levels. Consistently received high ratings.
- Managed a team of 4 administrators. Quickly turned a department in disarray with no budget controls into a smooth-running operation.
- Negotiated to reduce hotel costs 50%. Negotiated the construction of a classroom to Ambank specifications (which the hotel named the "Ambankgarden Room").
- Consulted with local management in Honduras and the Dominican Republic on new products and treasury services.

<u>**Vice President/Division Treasurer**</u> - **Venezuela**   1980 - 1981

Controlled the Treasury function in 4 countries (Venezuela, Aruba, Ecuador and Colombia). Assisted local management in developing and implementing a treasury strategy.

- To grow customer business, obtained permission from government authorities to engage in Fiduciary Business. This represents at least $2 million annual earnings, and is a major source of income.

<u>**Vice President/Cash and Currency Consultant**</u> - **Hong Kong**   1977 - 1980

Created and managed the cash- and currency-consulting function in Asia which was used by Multinational Customers as well as within Ambank.

- Consulted with approximately 50 Multinational companies.
- <u>Created 4 major new products which were successfully used in 8 countries.</u>

International Money Market - New York   prior to 1977
Corporate Systems Advisory Unit Head

Managed a team of 5 consultants and 2 administrators to design Foreign Exchange Exposure reports and perform international cash-management studies for multinational companies.

- Created AMBANKDATA/AMBANKRATE, a currency data base which 15 years later is being actively used by corporate clients as well as in-house.
- Completed 10 Cash Management Studies.

HOECHST ETECO, S.A. - Ecuador   **1964 - 1966**

Managed the Chemical and Dyestuff Department, supervising 2 salesmen. Tripled sales in 15 months.

LANGUAGES

Fluent in Spanish and German. Familiar with Portuguese and Dutch.

OTHER ACTIVITIES

Regularly lecture on currency management and cash management issues including
two appearances at Sloan School/MIT.

The Five O'Clock Club®

Donald Woodstone:Is a One-Page Résumé Better?

It wasn't entirely Don's fault. His résumé had been developed with the help of an outplacement firm. It is a typical historical résumé—it focuses on the past. It states each job and what he did in each.

Many people think a one-page résumé is more likely to get read. But Don's résumé proves that a short résumé is not necessarily better. His résumé was not presenting him the way he wanted to be presented. Don was not helped by a résumé that forced a lot of information into one completely unreadable page.

Don had been searching six months by the time I met him. He had not gotten in to see one person at a higher level than he was. He earned in excess of $200,000 and would be on payroll for for another full year (lucky him), but he was very discouraged.

Take a look at Don's old résumé. It is written in big, unreadable paragraphs. It is unscannable. No one will read a résumé like this. Remember: the reader has to get your message in only ten seconds. At the very least, the accomplishments should be bulleted to make them readable, and that alone will generally make the résumé longer than one page.

The old résumé has a summary, but it too is historical. For example, the second bullet brags that Don moved a data processing facility from New York to New Jersey. The reader will probably think: "We don't need to have a data processing center moved." It's not a selling point to the majority of his readers—so let's not mention it.

What is Don's real message here? It's that he saved the company $1 million —so that's what we mention on the new résumé. We highlight those things the reader might be interested in, which Don would like to do again. For example, he wanted to be positioned as a key member of the senior management team. This kind of thinking resulted in a strategic résumé.

Carefully study Don's résumé— before and after. It's a short one, so it won't take you long. Compare the old summary to the new one, and the write-up of each old job to the new write-up. It should give you a better feel for how you want to position yourself on *your* new résumé.

DONALD G. WOODSTONE

6 Cucumber Lane   Dorrisville, NJ 07000   (201) 555-6878

PROFILE

Senior Information Systems executive with significant record of accomplishments and experience in multiple industries, both domestic and international. An unbroken record of increasing responsibilities marked by measurable achievements in support of business growth and profitability objectives. Unique ability to successfully integrate and consolidate business functions into the mainstream organization. A successful leader and motivator of people who possesses the practical judgment to function successfully in centralized and decentralized business cultures. A consistent contributor to the attainment of business goals and maximizing operating efficiencies.

.   Consolidated into a single order-processing, customer-service operation 4 distinct businesses totaling $270 million in sales; this yielded a net annual savings of $1.4 million and enabled the business units to achieve additional synergies.

.   Saved $1 million annually by relocating an entire data processing organization from New York to New Jersey. Additional savings followed by the relocation of all support operations. This was accomplished without sacrifice to operating efficiency.

.   Created and implemented international financial reporting system for 72 worldwide locations. Provided real time delivery of financial data; continuous cash-flow monitoring, on-going assessment of profitability and consolidation of all data to generate financial statements.

CAREER SUMMARY

Senior Vice President, MIS   HARCOURT & SIMON, INC.   1984-Present

Organize and direct a Management Information Systems group with a $16.5 million operating budget; responsible for 135 employees. Establish policies and strategic direction; manage development of application systems, operation of the corporate center and all telecommunications. Responsible for data processing activities at 23 remote locations; consolidated 11 of these into the central location. Personally developed strategic and tactical plans for integration and consolidation of all newly acquired businesses. Consolidated all systems for payroll, general ledger, accounts payable, inventory accounting and accounts receivable into centralized applications. Reduced the number of Central Processing Units at the corporate center from four to one.

Group Director, MIS   ESTÉE LAUDER INC.   1978-1984

Developed MIS strategies and budgets for seven domestic and seven international companies in the Health Care Division, while overseeing the fulfillment of those plans at 29 domestic and international data processing centers. Initiated and developed worldwide financial reporting system. Represented division on corporate steering committee.

Director, Information Systems and Services   ROHRER INC.   1971-1978

Directed all systems development, computer operations and telecommunications at the corporate center and three division data processing centers. Promoted to Director in 1976 after managing the activities of a six-day 24-hour computer operation (71-76). Established procedures for introduction of new application and system software. Reorganized departments to improve service and reduce the required number of personnel.

Systems Manager/Analyst   NJ BELL TELEPHONE COMPANY   1957-1971

Various inter-departmental assignments with heavy exposure to data processing and business systems development. Progressed from sales trainee to Manager, Business Systems.

EDUCATION

B.S. in Economics   Villanova University   1957

Advanced Studies (Executive Programs):   Duke University   1974
                                                    Dartmouth College   1976

72

Donald G. Woodstone

6 Cucumber Lane
Dorrisville, N.J. 07000
201-555-6878

Senior Information Systems Executive

- **Manufacturing**
- **Health Services**
- **Telecommunications**
- **Pharmaceuticals**
- **Consumer Goods**
- **Publishing**

Key member of management team. Report directly to the COO or CEO.
Managed technological needs <u>for companies ranging from $250 million to over $1 billion.</u>

Rapidly Integrate/Consolidate Acquisitions/Businesses

- Consolidated the technologies and systems of <u>**over $1 billion in acquisitions.**</u>

- Consolidated <u>**4 distinct businesses**</u> totaling <u>**$270 million**</u> in sales into a single operation.
  - Net annual **savings of $1.4 million**.
  - Completely integrated within 8 months.
  - Enabled the business units to achieve significant additional savings.

- <u>**Saved $1 million annually on $5 million**</u> data processing budget—
  — with no sacrifice to operating efficiency.

- Developed **composite information base**.
  - Helped management see company as a logical, manageable organization and find other market opportunities that fit in.
  - Company avoided the problems so often associated with multiple acquisitions.

- Created <u>**international financial reporting system**</u> for <u>**73 locations worldwide.**</u>
  - Real-time delivery of financial data.
  - Continuous cash-flow monitoring.
  - On-going assessment of profitability.
  - Consolidation of financial statements.

Key Member of Senior Management Team

- Use technology to <u>**support and implement the strategic plans of the company**</u>.
- Developed 3-year strategic plan. Presented to corporate Board of Directors.
- Sensitive to profitability and enhancement of investment.

Develop Systems That Support Today's Business Environment

- Telecommunications network for <u>**32 locations;**</u> <u>**1400 terminals**</u> on-line to mainframe.
- Quickly develop/introduce new systems: use the latest methodologies and techniques.
- Developed security and contingency back-up plans that <u>**assure continuous operation**</u>.

<u>**A business manager and key member of the management team.**</u>
<u>**Use technology to achieve the strategic and profit plan of the organization**</u>
<u>**to allow companies to achieve a greater participation in their marketplace.**</u>

Strong hands-on, project-oriented business manager, strategic planner and leader.
Successful in centralized and decentralized business cultures.
Manage and control major development projects.

SENIOR VICE PRESIDENT, MIS
HARCOURT & SIMON, INC.   1984-Present

<u>Staff of 135</u>. $16.5 million operating budget.

- As key member of senior management team—
    - —set policies and direction to support and <u>implement overall strategic goals of company</u>.
    - —personally developed strategic and tactical plans for integration and <u>consolidation of all 39 newly acquired businesses</u>.

- <u>Developed methodology to quickly consolidate all companies</u> for payroll, general ledger, accounts payable, inventory accounting & accounts receivable into centralized applications.
    - <u>All went smoothly</u>.   <u>No adverse impact</u> on any of the companies involved.
    - <u>Company saved $35 million</u>.

- Manage application development, computer operations and all telecommunications.
    - Also responsible for data processing at 23 remote locations. Consolidated 11 centrally.
    - Use the latest systems-development methodologies and techniques (Expert Systems, CASE technologies, CD-ROM).
        - For <u>quick development and introduction of new systems.</u>
        - <u>Helps company stay competitive and on top of a dynamically growing organization.</u>

- Closed 3 data processing centers with no adverse impact.
    - <u>Saved company $1 million annually on $5 million</u> data processing budget.

- <u>Developed management personnel</u> so they operated effectively and independently.

GROUP DIRECTOR
ESTÉE LAUDER, INC.   1978-1984

- Managed MIS plans, budgets & activities at <u>22 domestic and 7 international centers</u> (230 people).
- <u>Managed 7 domestic and 7 international companies.</u>
- Initiated and developed <u>world-wide financial reporting system</u>.
- Respresented division on corporate steering committee.

DIRECTOR, INFORMATION SYSTEMS AND SERVICES
ROHRER, INC.   1971-1978

Directed all systems development, computer operations and telecommunications at the <u>corporate center and 3 division data processing centers.</u>
- Established procedures for "problem-free" introduction of new application and system software.
- Improved service and reduced the required number of personnel.

SYSTEMS MANAGER/ANALYST
NJ BELL TELEPHONE COMPANY   1957-1971

Regularly promoted. Progressed from sales trainee to Manager, Business Systems.

EDUCATION

B.S., Economics, Villanova University, 1957
Executive Program, Duke University, 1974
Executive Program, Dartmouth College, 1976

George Lucas: Getting Out of a Dead Market

Why not go out on a limb?
That's where the fruit is.
Will Rogers

The earth is a place to live in, where we must put up with sights, with sounds, with smells, too, by Jove!—breathe dead hippo, so to speak, and not be contaminated. And there, don't you see? Your strength comes in, the faith in your ability for the digging of unostentatious holes to bury the stuff in—your power of devotion, not to yourself, but to an obscure, backbreaking business.

Joseph Conrad, *Heart of Darkness*

George had spent seventeen years selling a certain financial-services product. His entire career was based on it. Now that product no longer existed, and the clients he had developed over the years would no longer be a help to him. George would have to start from scratch in another area. When he did his Seven Stories Exercise, a number of things became clear:

• He liked to sell rather than simply manage salespeople. He wanted to be a "producing manager" in his next position.

• A repeated theme was that he had taken businesses from zero and had grown them into something substantial. George was going to have to do this again—but in a field very different from the one he had been in. We decided to make this the theme in his new résumé. To make it stand out even more, we underlined it in the summary and emphasized it throughout his résumé: **Proven record of building customer relations and business revenues in a short time frame**.

• One other consideration was that in George's industry, there were many unsavory people. George wanted to work for someone ethical. Therefore, the last line of his summary statement informs them which side of the fence he is on. The personal information was added at the end to let them know that he is a good family man, retired from the Marines, and so on.

George found himself a new job that not only paid the high base he had made before, but he also got an equity position in the new company. What's more, his search took him only two months. A résumé that positioned him properly helped his search along, and his background in an outmoded area was no longer a liability.

GEORGE LUCAS
47 Dublin Street
New York, New York 11000
Business: 212-555-1111
Home: 212-333-4444

BUSINESS EXPERIENCE:

1986-Present	Manager U.S. Government Securities Sales and Trading, GlitzBank, London.
1983-1986	President GlitzBank Securities Markets Inc., a NASD registered broker dealer and wholly owned subsidiary of GlitzBank operating U.S. government securities sales offices in five major U.S. cities.
1979-1983	Salesman and Manager of GlitzBank Mortgage-Backed Securities Sales Team covering top tier U.S. thrifts and mortgage-banking companies.
1976-1979	Sales Manager for GlitzBank Private Banking Services for high-net-worth individual clients in the New York Metropolitan region.
1973-1976	Manager GlitzBank Investment Selection Service and IRA Rollover products ($25MM equity portfolio).
1971-1973	Relationship Manager, GlitzBank Private Banking Dept. ($20MM loan portfolio).

EDUCATION: B.S., Finance, Rutgers University, 1966;
Credit Analysis Program, GlitzBank, 1972;
T.E.P., Darden School, University of Virginia, 1979;
Registered Series 3,7, and Municipal Securities Principal

PERSONAL: U.S. Naval Aviator, Major USMCR retired
Married, 4 children
Excellent Health
Hobbies - include golf, skiing, shooting

GEORGE LUCAS

47 Dublin Street
New York, New York 11000

Home: 212-333-4444
Business: 212-555-1111

SUMMARY OF QUALIFICATIONS

17 years' experience with GlitzBank in sales of financial services. 8 years in the fixed-income market covering major institutional customers in the U.S. and Europe. **Proven record of building customer relations and business revenues in a short time frame.** A strong producing manager who is demanding but reasonable and easy to deal with. Sets high standards of customer service, integrity and professionalism.

PROFESSIONAL EXPERIENCE

GLITZBANK   1971-Present

Institutional Bond Sales   1988-Present
Team Leader

> o Mortgage-Backed Securities coverage of major U.S. mortgage bankers.
> o U.S. governments, options and MBS sales to key London customers.

GlitzBank Investment Bank, London   1986-1988
Producing Manager, U.S. Government Securities Sales and Trading

> o Directed 6 salespeople and 2 traders (London and Zurich).
> o Distributed government and MBS to customers in Europe and Middle East.

Regional Sales Manager   1983-1986

> o In charge of five U.S. institutional sales offices - **60 people.**
> o Distributed government, municipal and MBS across the U.S.
> o **Grew the business from $2 to $15 million in revenues in a 3-year period.**
> o Made GlitzBank the first bank dealer with an effective regional office network.

GlitzBank Mortgage-Backed Securities   1979-1983
Producing Manager

> o Personally opened up ten top-tier U.S. thrifts and mortgage-banking institutions for GlitzBank.
> o Created a business and customer base that didn't exist for GlitzBank prior to 1980.
> o **Grew volume from 0 to $3 billion in 2 years**.

GlitzBank Private Banking Services   1977-1979
Sales Manager

> o Directed 5 salespeople marketing trust and investment services to high-net-worth individual clients in the New York metropolitan region.

Business and Portfolio Manager   1973-1976

- o Directed investment decisions on individual accounts aggregating to a $25-million equity portfolio.
- o Designed and launched GlitzBank's IRA Rollover and Keogh products.
- o Supervised advertising, direct-mail and telemarketing promotional efforts.

GlitzBank Private Banking Department   1971-1973
Relationship Manager

- o Cross-sold and delivered banking and investment services to high-net-worth individual clients.
- o Built a $20-million loan portfolio.

EDUCATION

B.S., Finance, Rutgers University, 1966
Credit Analysis Program, GlitzBank, 1972
Executive Program, Darden School, University of Virginia, 1979
Registered Series 3,7 and Municipal Securities Principal.

PERSONAL

Naval Aviator, Major USMCR retired
Married, 4 children
Excellent health
Hobbies include golf, skiing, shooting

Norman Neumann's Résumé: Strategy, not Consistency

Norman called me in distress from California. He was not proud of his performance in the last three years, and felt that he had failed. He wanted a résumé that would exclude that time.

We did the entire project over the phone. It took about six hours total to talk about his situation and background, and complete the résumé—which did *not* hide what he had done during the past three years.

Most of the people I work with have had great careers—until just a little while before I meet them. That's why they are calling me. Things are negative. They want to move on, and are not sure how to position their present situation.

In Norman's case, my business background came in handy. He told me what had happened during the past three years. The way he described it, it seemed terrible. After taking many notes, I noticed the positives. Often, ambitious people do not fulfill the goals they had in mind, and thus consider themselves failures. They discount everything that they have done—even the positives. Yet, a person has often done something worthwhile, has learned much from a failing situation, and can market that experience. It simply requires a different spin.

I said to him, "Norman, here's what it sounds like to me: you did a great job growing the company, but it ran a bit ahead of your working capital. When you realized this, you hustled around to find someone to conduct a friendly takeover of the firm. These people liked and respected you so well that they wanted to keep you on to run that company and another company of theirs as well. Is that right?"

Norman couldn't believe his ears. "Everything you said is true! But I haven't been looking at it that way." Later, he said, " For three years, I've been very depressed. Now I feel like a new person."

Many of you may be in a similar situation. You are glum. Perhaps it looks as if you have done a bad job. Maybe you have. But chances are, there is a good explanation for what happened. If you can get some distance and look at it with new eyes, you may be on the road to improving the predicament you are now in.

Norman's résumé is a good example of many of the things I preach. First of all, he did the Seven Stories Exercise so it would become clear which parts we should highlight. The stories gave a good overview of his career—what he was good at and what he was proud of.

Norman originally wanted two résumés: one he could use in the fashion industry where he had spent his working life, and another in case he had to look outside the industry, given its present condition. Actually, as so often happens, one résumé served both purposes.

Now let's take a look at Norman's résumé in detail.

Norman's summary positions him as a person who grows profitable businesses. This is in stark contrast to his old résumé, which made him look like a manufacturing expert.

In real life, Norman's résumé is on one piece of paper (17" across x 11" down) folded—so it comes out 8.5" x 11". It's four pages long, but it looks like a booklet. The summary appears on the front. Page 2 appears on the inside left, page 3 on the inside right, and page 4 on the back.

"Hiding" Three Years

Page 2 contains the years he wanted to hide. If we had had a shorter summary on page 1, part of this time-frame would have appeared on page 1, and that would not have been good. Another strategy would have been to cut this part very short.

But I felt Norman had a lot to brag about during those years, and I didn't want to short-change him. The most important story in his résumé is on page 3. Therefore, page 2 contains a lot of information. It contains so much that the reader's eye tends to skip right across to page 3. The second page was made crowded intentionally.

Highlighting the Main Story

On page 2, the word PRESIDENT is meant to pop out before the reader's eye goes on to page 3. On page 3, the story is that Norman started this company. The main message runs down the center of the page: Took the Company from 0 to $13 million . . . from Business Start-up . . . and Financing . . . to Business Development . . . and the running of Day-to-Day Operations. That's the main message.

There are subordinate messages too. For example, under Business Start-up, the subordinate message is "Hired all key sales . . . " This message is underlined because it is so important, yet it

does not detract from the main message. There are other subordinate messages. For example, under Financing, the words "creative financing techniques" are highlighted—but not enough to detract from the main message. Under Business Development the subordinate message is "7500 women at the Republican National Convention." And under the last section, the subordinate message is "skilled negotiator."

Full of Inconsistencies

Now take a look at all the job titles and company names. On page 2, the first job has no title at all. That's because the job title there would have detracted from the main message, which is that Norman runs entire companies. The word "president" in the middle of that page is highlighted. At the top of page 2, the company name is underlined and bolded. The company name at the middle of the page, however, is neither underlined nor bolded, to deemphasize it.

On page 3, the company name is in caps because this company name is prestigious (the real one, that is—this one is fictitious). On page 4, the job title that sticks out most is "president." The other company names or job titles are highlighted as appropriate.

I can assure you that no one asks why a certain title or company name is highlighted. It's obvious why. And it isn't offensive, is it?

Various but Appropriate Formats

There is a further inconsistency in this résumé. It has four pages, and each one is in a *completely different format*. Each page is formatted in a way that is appropriate for the message we are trying to convey on that page. The summary is very different from page 2, which is different from page 3. Page 4 ap-

proaches a more normal résumé format, but there are still inconsistencies in the titles and company names.

We are trying to tell a story. And we use the format that best does this. No one looks at this résumé and notices that there are four different formats.

Our Main Goal: Get the Message Across

Decide what message you are trying to tell. Does your story pop out? Or are you the type who records your history and leaves it up to the reader to figure out its significance? It is your job to decide how you want to position yourself, and then go to the trouble of doing it.

The result is a résumé that speaks for you, and an interview situation where they wind up asking you about the parts you want to emphasize.

There's no reason to have your present negative situation color the entire rest of your background. The résumé proudly presents your experience so that the reader recognizes your accomplishments and your potential within the marketplace.

Norman S. Neumann

5341 Churchcross Road
Los Angeles, California 90074
213-555-7220
213-555-0876 (message)

Summary of Qualifications

Senior General Management Executive with over 20 years of P&L and functional management experience. Consistently **grow profitable businesses from 0 to millions in a short time frame**.

Areas of Expertise include:

- **Overall Business Management**
- **Start-up Operations**
- **Financing**
- **New Business Development**
- **Sales and Marketing Management**
- **Manufacturing and Operations Management**
- **Merchandising and Cost Control**
- **Management/Planning/Restructuring**
- **Negotiations with Landlords, Labor Unions and Vendors**

- A strong **start-up manager**. A troubleshooter and problem-solver. Successfully open up new companies. Expert in situations requiring high growth.

- Know every area of the business operations and the products down to the details.

- **Attract top-level sales and management teams on a national level.**

- Well-known, respected, and trusted in the industry as a top-of-the-table negotiator.

- **Strong working relationships at all levels in national chain and specialty stores** such as Neiman Marcus, Saks Fifth Avenue, Bergdorf Goodman, Lord & Taylor, I. Magnin & Company, Bullocks Wilshire, Robinsons, and Martha.

- Motivate executives as well as store personnel to back products and **insure success**.

- **Strong public image**. Inspire a high level of confidence.

- Strong presentation skills: to 7500 women at the Republican National Convention, formal fashion shows for Saks and Neiman Marcus, and TV talk-show appearances.

- Highly experienced and successful in putting together National Co-op Advertising Programs in publications such as *Harper's, Vogue, W, Town and Country*, and *Connoisseur*.

- Senior-level experience in working with **Japanese-owned companies**.

**A business-builder: able to produce high-quality merchandise,
motivate a sales force, and develop long-term relationships
with national chains and specialty stores of the highest quality.**

Outgoing, friendly, intense, ambitious, well-traveled, straightforward "people-person."

Wearmagic, Inc. 1992-present

Manage two divisions: one start-up division and one turnaround of a problem division.

- **Reorganized and redirected a problem business** (R.L. Meyer Division).
  - Restored balance and revenue growth.
  - Now a $4-million business. Projected revenues of $6 million for 1990.

- In November, 1988, **developed and introduced the Koki Selman label**, a high-priced designer line of ladies' suits, costumes and dresses.
  - Project growth **from 0 to $3 million within first 12 months**.
  - Achieved **national product exposure** for Koki Selman **at a very low cost**. In catalogs such as Bergdorf's, Montaldo's, Talbot's, I. Magnin, and Neiman Marcus.
  - Implemented cooperative advertising programs.
  - **One of the top five showrooms in America.**

PRESIDENT 1990-1992
R.L. Meyer, Inc. (Later acquired by Wearmagic, Inc.)

Joined company in mid-1990, after it had loss for fiscal year just ended of $1.3 million sales. Company had antiquated plant and equipment, no equity, and a work force of 42—primarily workers on social security. **Immediately developed and implemented plan to turn around performance:**

- Strengthened financial and operating controls;
- **Negotiated favorable terms with a national factor and a substantially larger banking line of credit**;
- Revamped product line; To control costs, reorganized production operations;
- Increased prices by 30 to 40% to reflect actual costs that had never been analyzed;
- Started a sales force where none previously existed. Established sales organizations in New York, Chicago and Los Angeles;
- Broadened distribution and **increased sales to $6 million within one year**;
- **Negotiated major labor contract concessions**;
- Attracted large national catalogs and retail operations such as Talbot's, I. Magnin, Neiman Marcus, Saks Fifth Avenue, Bergdorf Goodman, Nordstrom.

As a consequence, sales increased dramatically. To attract the necessary long-term capital to support increased business, took the following actions:

- Initiated discussions with prospective equity partners.
- Took advantage of legal reorganization provisions.
- Developed a workable plan for reorganization and found purchasers for a friendly takeover.

Company became and is now a division of Wearmagic, Inc. Became responsible for:

- the continued growth of R. L. Meyer, and
- the start-up of another, now highly successful, division.

Stockholder/Vice President/Secretary 1982-1990

JORDAN HANES, INC.

Founded company with Jordan Hanes, designer. Established an exclusive manufacturing business of fine women's apparel. Collection of day and evening wear retailing from $250 to $1600.

Took the Company from 0 to $13 million, giving it a national reputation for quality and leadership.

Managed the entire business side of the company from:

Business Start-up . . .

- Established company from its inception: Procured leases, all necessary business licenses, Dun's number, and listing with Dun and Bradstreet.
- Organized, contracted and executed construction of facilities including all project management, and negotiation of budgeting and costing with all manufacturing contractors.
- **Hired all key sales and management personnel. All are still in place today.**

and Financing . . .

- Built a solid financial reputation on a national and international level.
- Used **creative financing techniques** to obtain favorable financing during start-up as well as during extraordinary growth. Received backing of national commercial factors.
- Secured lease in prime area of L.A. for only one-third of market rate.
- Through financing, increased capitalization by 40%; this increased profits by 10%.

to Business Development . . .

- Established and maintained a customer base of 803 active accounts including: Neiman Marcus, Saks Fifth Avenue, Bergdorf Goodman, Lord & Taylor, I. Magnin, Bullocks Wilshire, Robinsons, Martha.
- Staged 150-200 fashion shows, seminars and charity events including shows for the finest stores in America, and for **7500 women at the Republican National Convention**.
- Ran national clinics, fashion shows and trunk shows.
- Handled all advertising and promotional functions; negotiated and contracted with media/publcations.

and the running of all Day-to-Day Operations.

- Created, planned and implemented company fringe-benefit plan. Worked with corporate attorneys and accountants. Obtained government approval of pension and profit-sharing plans and tax-effective benefits for employees as well as executives.
- A **skilled negotiator** with vendors, suppliers and leasing companies. Obtained the lowest available cost while maintaining quality.
- Installed efficient administrative systems and controls that are still being used today.
- Set up and oversaw an efficient manufacturing production system that insured quality-control inspection and scheduling.
- Developed all procedure manuals and administrative responsibilities, shipping/receiving, importing and inventory control.

Key Account Sales Consultant   1979-1982
Young Stuff, Incorporated

- **Starting with a territory of 0, developed sales into $6 million**, which accounted for 1/3 of total company billing.

La Milagros Cordero, a **national sales organization**   1978-1979

- A start-up operation.
- With partner, grew company **from 0 to $20 million**, sales offfices in New York and Los Angeles, and 11 salesmen.
- Negotiated exclusive rights to market in the U.S. and Mexico. Upscale, high-quality Spanish merchandise which included the finest-quality leather and suedes.

PRESIDENT   1972-1978
Mr. Chris for Men (high-quality men's clothing and furnishings)

- Company had been heavily in debt. **Within one year**:
  - removed all debt,
  - increased volume 120%
  - and square footage by 100%.

- **Made company highly profitable** with a volume of $4 million and 3 locations.
  - Made company cash-heavy and financially secure.
  - Received backing of national and local factors.
  - Through bank, negotiated substantial and favorable SBA loan for capital improvements.

- **Negotiated lease(s):**
  - that are still in place today and are producing substantial revenues.
  - with largest shopping center in America.
  - with major motion picture studio's real estate division.

Direct Sales Agent   1968-1972
John Rose California

- Assigned the company's smallest territory.
- **Starting from virtually 0, increased sales to over $3 million**.
- This accounted for **50% of the company's total sales**.

EDUCATION

B.S., Business Administration, The University of Southern California
Graduate, General Studies, The Mercersberg Academy

Craig Brown: Trying to Make a Career Change

A History of Trying to Make a Career Change

Craig Brown has lived in London for the past four years. He went there to get out of operations, but he wound up in another operations job.

In fact, Craig has a history of not being able to get out of whatever field he is in. When he was younger, he was a rocket scientist. Craig was very competent, but he wanted to make a change. So he moved to Israel, and what do you suppose he wound up doing there? That's right. Rocket science.

When he returned to the States, a friend found him a responsible job at First Express. He did a great job, but was itchy to get out on his own. He became a partner in a clothing business that was not doing very well. Craig turned the company around (although it was difficult to tell that from his old résumé).

Then he had a series of odd jobs, including running his own business, which was the most exciting thing he had ever done. When he was pushed out by organized crime, he turned to his old friend and got back into First Express—into an operations role.

Why Craig Has Problems

Part of Craig's problem is that he's too eager to get the next job. Making a major career move takes long-term planning and persistence. But he has also been held back by the way he has positioned himself.

Like most people, Craig has had some experience in the area where he would like to head his career. But his résumé was historical. All it did was present the jobs he had held and tell what he did in those jobs.

A Strategic Résumé

We made his résumé strategic and forward-looking. He did his Seven Stories Exercise so we could figure out the areas he would enjoy most in the future. We highlighted those areas in his résumé.

His new résumé goes a long way toward positioning him for a role that will lead him out of operations. It speaks on his behalf and highlights those accomplishments that show more than his operations skills.

Look Your Level

Although he was earning in the $150,000 range, his old résumé made him look low-level. His new résumé makes him look his executive level.

Add Zip and Direction to Your Search

His revamped résumé gave new life to his job search. It positioned him for the kind of things he wanted to do next, and showed how his personality was effective on the job, even though he acted very laid back in the interviews.

Senior managers, especially those who are technically oriented, do not understand the need for résumés that position them. They feel their actions should speak for themselves. But a résumé is part of your presentation, just as much as the way you are dressed and your speech are. And it speaks for you in your absence, if a manager passes on your résumé to someone else.

Finally, your résumé should predispose the hiring manager to see you in a certain way. Then all you have to do in the interview is live up to the positive expectations he or she has--rather than overcome the negative expectations caused by a bad résumé.

By the way, this résumé got Craig in to see many people who refused to see him before. He quickly landed an appropriate job.

CRAIG I. BROWN

Darden Flat
3 Upper Trevordale Gardens
London W9 9BG England

Residence: 011-44-71-555-3784
Business: 011-44-71-555-5044

SUMMARY

Proven track record of performance, especially in the area of creative and time-critical problem solving, increased profit statements and proven relationship management. Strong commitment to customer service and management by objectives through the establishment of critical elements for personnel performance. Excellent customer relations and supervisory skills, having been operating partner in own manufacturing business. International investment-banking operations, engineering and business background provide transferable skill base applicable to all areas of business. Able to interact with all facets of business environment.

EXPERIENCE

FIRST EXPRESS   1981-Present
Vice President

Director
INFOMATICS LTD (FIRST EXPRESS SUBSIDIARY)

Responsible for the production, financial, administrative and legal and regulatory aspects of an embryonic data-broadcast business.
- Successfully established or rebuilt relationships with customers and suppliers.
- Effectively managed the on-time production, delivery of the first commercial product.
- Formulated and implemented financial, production and business controls and reporting.

Senior Country Operations Officer   1986-1989
UK SPECIAL BANK

Staff of 600 operating and technical personnel and a $48-million expense base. Operated in an international environment, providing support for all local and international origination, distribution and trading of fixed income, treasury and equity products.
- contributed to profitability of the bank through significant reduction in expense base:
  - Reduced expenses by $8 million.
  - Reduced staff by 200.
  - Maintained or improved service levels and corrected control deficiencies.
- Developed senior management personnel to the point where they operated effectively on an independent basis.

Head of Operations   1981-1986
NORTH AMERICAN DIVISION

Staff of over 500 operating personnel and a $24-million expense base. Provided support of all facets of fixed-income origination, distribution and trading with gross money movements in excess of $20 billion daily.
- Managed the development and implementation of the processing support experiencing:
  - 20% annual transaction volume increase.
  - 50% annual product growth.
- Formulated strategic operational plans.
  - Met business needs despite dynamic growth.

<u>General Manager</u>   1980-1981
UNIVERSAL INDUSTRIAL EQUIPMENT COMPANY

General Manager of a medium-size manufacturing company (subsidiary of large conglomerate).
Responsible for operations and general business planning.
- Reported directly to President of the parent company.
- Increased sales over 100% with a 30% net profit increase.
- Oversaw and monitored performance of 45 professional and support personnel. Identified
  and eliminated waste and duplication.
- Planned and established manufacturing/distribution cycle to satisfy customers' needs.

Management Consultant   1977-1980

Provided consulting services to a variety of manufacturing, wholesale distribution & service
companies. Specialized in manufacturing problems, especially workflow analysis, personnel
and sales. Created and directed implementation of systems and operations to maximize profits.

<u>Vice President</u>   1974-1977
MONIKER CLOTHES, INC., PHILADELPHIA, PA.

As partner in manufacturing company for top-of-line men's clothing, was responsible for both
daily operation and general business plan. Managed daily performance of 320 professional and
support personnel. Analyzed manufacturing cycle to cut overhead and increase profit margin.
Responsible for cash flow, including factoring of accounts receivables. Established lines of
credit and capital base. Excellent labor-management relations experience in dealing with a
strong and active union. Sold business.

<u>Assistant Vice President</u>   1971-1974
FIRST EXPRESS, New York, NY

Responsible for analysis and systems solutions to Data Center/Operations interface problems.
Developed and implemented management information systems resulting in elimination of two-year
backlog, reduction in accounts receivable and 25% expense reduction. Managed 150 professional
and support personnel. Responsible for establishing budget, performance and workflow objectives in the securities area.

AEROSPACE ENGINEER   1959-1971

Upon being awarded a B.M.E. Degree, worked in a variety of engineering and engineering management capacities including: Professor of Engineering, Senior Research Engineer, Design Engineer and Experimental Test Engineer. Work involved technical supervision, analysis of problems and customer contact at all levels of management. Excellent data processing management
experience.

EDUCATION

B.M.E. Degree: Mechanical Engineering, 1959
Georgia Institute of Technology, Atlanta, GA

M.Sc. Degree: Aeronautical Engineering, 1971
Israel Institute of Technology, Haifa, Israel

Craig I. Brown

Darden Flat
3 Upper Trevordale Gardens
London W9 9BG England
Residence: 011-44-1-555-3784
Business: 011-44-1-555-5044

This résumé positions him as a Senior Executive who knows more than operations--he knows how to manage a business as well as relationships.

SUMMARY OF QUALIFICATIONS

He likes action --so we'll use "start-ups and turnarounds" as the theme of the résumé.

Senior General Management Executive.
Manage the start-up and turnaround of relationships, products, companies.

Areas of Expertise include:

Stresses areas he thinks he'd like to be in next.

- Overall Business Management
- Relationship Management
- Market Analysis/Sales Management
- Management/Planning /Restructuring
- Managing Fast-Growth Situations

- International Operations/Global Expansions
- Strategic Planning
- Negotiation Skills
- Financial, Business and Production Controls
- Developing Senior Management Personnel

- Strong Start-up and Turnaround Manager

- **Manage companies and relationships with an entrepreneurial style and entrepreneurial experience**.
  - Successfully open up new companies.
  - Straighten out existing companies and relationships.
  - Expert in situations requiring high growth and relationship management.
  - A troubleshooter and problem-solver.
- Know every area of the business operations and the products down to the details.
- **Strong strategic vision** coupled with overall business sense **and attention to details**.
- A quick thinker:
  - Manage "unmanageable" customers.
  - Solve "unsolvable" business problems.
- Manage professional staffs ranging from 150 to 600.
  - **Reduced staff** from 800 to 600 **while** maintaining or **improving service levels**.
  - Set the direction for large groups.
  - **Calmly spur the management team to action**.
- Strong presentation skills.
- An international manager:
  - Lived and worked in three countries.
  - Managed international businesses.

In interviews, he is laid back. We want the reader to know that he spurs on his team —but in a calm manner.

A global business manager, strategic thinker, and negotiator.
A creative and time-critical problem-solver.
Resolve customer complaints. Develop long-term relationships.

Ethical, straightforward, action-oriented, unflappable.
Operate well under pressure. Solve crises quickly.
Respected and trusted as a top-of-the-table negotiator.

All of the résumés highlight personality traits. They need to know not only what you did, but how you went about it.

Craig I. Brown

Darden Flat
3 Upper Trevordale Gardens
London W9 9BG England
Residence: 011-44-1-555-3784
Business: 011-44-1-555-5044

SUMMARY OF QUALIFICATIONS

Senior General Management Executive.
Manage the start-up and turnaround of relationships, products, companies.

Areas of Expertise include:

- **Overall Business Management**
- **Relationship Management**
- **Market Analysis/Sales Management**
- **Management/Planning /Restructuring**
- **Managing Fast-Growth Situations**
- **International Operations/Global Expansions**
- **Strategic Planning**
- **Negotiation Skills**
- **Financial, Business and Production Controls**
- **Developing Senior Management Personnel**
- **Strong Start-up and Turnaround Manager**

- **Manage companies and relationships with an entrepreneurial style and entrepreneurial experience**.
  - Successfully open up new companies.
  - Straighten out existing companies and relationships.
  - Expert in situations requiring high growth and relationship management.
  - A troubleshooter and problem-solver.

- Know every area of the business operations and the products down to the details.

- **Strong strategic vision** coupled with overall business sense **and attention to details**.

- A quick thinker:
  - Manage "unmanageable" customers.
  - Solve "unsolvable" business problems.

- Manage professional staffs ranging from 150 to 600.
  - **Reduced staff** from 800 to 600 **while** maintaining or **improving service levels**.
  - Set the direction for large groups.
  - **Calmly spur the management team to action**.

- Strong presentation skills.

- An international manager:
  - Lived and worked in three countries.
  - Managed international businesses.

A global business manager, strategic thinker, and negotiator.
A creative and time-critical problem-solver.
Resolve customer complaints. Develop long-term relationships.

Ethical, straightforward, action-oriented, unflappable.
Operate well under pressure. Solve crises quickly.
Respected and trusted as a top-of-the-table negotiator.

FIRST EXPRESS 1981-present
Vice President

DIRECTOR, Informatics Ltd. (FIRST EXPRESS subsidiary)

Key player in this **embryonic** data processing **business**. Managed all production, financial, administrative and legal aspects.

- Successfully established or **rebuilt relationships** with customers and suppliers.
- Effectively managed the on-time production and delivery of the **first commercial product**.
- Formulated and implemented financial, production & business controls, & reporting.

SENIOR COUNTRY OPERATIONS OFFICER, U.K. 1986-1989

Staff of 600 operating and technical personnel. **$48 million** expense base.

- An **international environment**. Provided support for all local and international origination, distribution and trading of fixed income, treasury and equity products.
- **Increased profitability** through significant reduction in expense base:
  - Reduced expenses by $8 million.
  - Reduced staff by 200 yet . . .
    . . . maintained or improved service levels and
    . . . corrected control deficiencies.
- Developed senior-management personnel so they operated effectively and independently.

HEAD OF OPERATIONS, North American Division 1981-1986

Staff of 550. **$24 million** expense base.

Formulated strategic operational plans. Met business needs despite **dynamic growth**.

- Supported all facets of origination, distribution and trading.
- Gross money movements in excess of **$20 billion daily**.
- Managed the development and implementation of the processing support:
  - transaction **volume increased 20%** annually.
  - product growth of 50% annually.

GENERAL MANAGER, Universal Industrial Equipment Company 1980-1981

Managed overall business planning as well as day-to-day operations of a medium-size manufacturing company (subsidiary of large conglomerate).

- Reported directly to President of the parent company.
- **Increased sales** over 100%. **Increased net profits** 30%.
- Satisfied customers' needs through the planning and establishment of a manufacturing and distribution cycle.

Management Consultant 1977-1980
To a variety of service, manufacturing, and wholesale distribution companies.

- Specialized in manufacturing problems, especially in **sales, workflow analysis, and personnel**.
- Created and directed implementation of systems and operations to maximize profits.

VICE PRESIDENT and PARTNER, Moniker Clothes, Inc.   1974-1977

<u>**Turned around company**</u> . . .

> . . . that had been operating at a loss, and had the highest expense base in the industry.

- <u>**Developed**</u> general and ongoing <u>**business plan**</u> to run the company.

- <u>**Managed**</u> daily operations. <u>**Staff of 320**</u> professional and support personnel.

- Analyzed manufacturing cycle to cut overhead and <u>**increase profit margin**</u>.
    - Responsible for cash flow, including factoring of accounts receivable.
    - Established lines of credit and capital base.

- <u>**Negotiated**</u> with a strong and active union. Maintained excellent labor-management relations.

    Sold the business.

DEPARTMENT HEAD, First Express   1971-1974

Managed <u>**3 departments**</u>. <u>**Staff of 150**</u> professional and support personnel.

- Established budget, performance and workflow objectives.

- <u>**Turned around**</u> an area that had major operational and relationship problems:
    - Quickly analyzed the problem and developed concept to solve it.
    - Developed an MIS system that resulted in the <u>**elimination of two-year backlog.**</u>
    - <u>**Within 3 weeks**</u>, stopped the growth in the backlog.
    - Reduced accounts receivables (many of which were 2 or 3 years old), and
    - Reduced expenses by 25%.

- Developed and delivered <u>**presentation to division head**</u> on new approach to company business. Later adopted at large.

AEROSPACE ENGINEER   1959-1971

Worked in a variety of engineering and engineering management capacities:

- Worked on <u>**Saturn, Mariner and Voyager rockets**</u>.
- <u>**Advised NASA**</u> and delivered presentation to them.
- Presented to technical groups around the country.
- Supervised technical staff. Analyzed complex problems.
- <u>**Customer contact at all levels of management**</u>.
- Excellent data processing management experience.

EDUCATION

M.Sc., Aeronautical Engineering, 1971
Israel Institute of Technology

B.M.E., Mechanical Engineering, 1959
Georgia Institute of Technology

Verna Hafner: Repositioned as a Generalist

In making our work a gift to the world, in making it an expression of our love for life, for God, and for our fellow man, we fulfill our highest potential, our most beautiful destiny as human beings.
Michael Lynberg, *The Path With Heart*

Summing up her career in her autobiography, she said: "My attitude had never changed. I cannot imagine feeling lackadaisical about a perfomance. I treat each encounter as a matter of life and death. The one important thing I have learned over the years is the difference between taking one's work seriously and taking one's self seriously. The first is imperative and the second disastrous."
Dame Margot Fonteyn,
Obituary in *The New York Times*

Verna had become known as a guru in a very small specialty area. The chances of finding another position in that specialty were slim, and even if they had not been, Verna was ready for a change. She had worked many years, expected to work many more, and so wanted to reposition herself-- as someone who could run different kinds of businesses. Therefore, her résumé positioned her as a generalist who had run businesses.

Before Verna went on interviews, she studied in depth the industries of the people she approached. She was extremely knowledgeable in her conversations with senior management. She sounded so authoritative that it never became an issue that Verna had not worked in those industries.

Most general managers have a sub-specialty, such as marketing, finance, operations, or whatever. If you are positioning yourself as a generalist, consider letting your reader know your subspecialty. In Verna's case, it was marketing.

The following résumé is on 11" x 17" paper, folded. The front page is a summary so that the reader cannot possibly see the specialty area Verna was in (on page 2), but instead gets a picture of her as a generalist.

When the reader opens up the résumé booklet, the expanse of Verna's experience is spread across the middle two pages. Verna's generalist perspective is again reinforced, broken down by the functional areas she managed, such as marketing.

On the other hand, if Verna had wanted to present herself as a specialist, the specialty areas would have been in her headline. It's as easy as that.

VERNA HAFNER
109 Vilrna Hill Road
Ann Arbor, MI 49403
Home: (555) 468-4907
Work: (555) 820-9361

Summary of Qualifications

A senior global business executive.
A marketer who successfully starts up and turns around
complex businesses, products and relationships.

Areas of Expertise include:

- Overall Business Management
- Strategic Planning
- Product Development
- Technological innovation
- Sales & Marketing Management
- Operations Management
- Relationship Management
- Quality Management
- Public Relations & Advertising Programs

- <u>**Strong Start up and Turnaround Manager.**</u>
  - Successfully started up a <u>**business**</u> which <u>**had languished for 5+ years**</u>.
  - Grew it from annual revenues of $2 million per year to $68 million after 5 years.
- Industry expert known and respected globally:
  - <u>**International conference speaker**</u>.
  - Developed and delivered seminars, gave interviews, appeared on TV and radio globally to sell company's products, services and expertise.
- <u>**Creative developer of Quality Marketing, Sales and Advertising Programs**</u> regarded as "the best" in the industry.
- Repositioned company in the competitive arena <u>**from a nonplayer to a major contender**</u>.
- <u>**Developed an "upscaled" and more diversified business team**</u> by revamping and expanding the organizational structure and resources.
- Senior-level experience in <u>**working with executives of multi-national companies from 27 countries**</u>.

A business or product builder.
Expert at creating and positioning complex strategies in diversified markets.

An agent of change.
Global traveller; caring; action-oriented; direct; integrity plus; a risk taker.

AMROCK, INC.
Vice President, *Commerical Products Business Manager*   1984 - Present

Full P&L responsibility for Global business

**Took over business that had no strategy or business plans,
had failed audits, poor performance, problem accounts, fragmented organization,
personnel problems and revenues of $2 million**

Developed it into a $68-million business with a presence in 27 countries.

Business Start-up

- Implemented Global Feasibility Study. Assessed short- and long-term revenue opportunity, competitive environment and receptiveness of Amrock's re-entry into the marketplace.
- Established 5-year strategic direction and product plan.
- Increased and upgraded staff from 35 to 60 to match marketplace needs.
- Installed Core System as basis for business acceleration.
- Organized, contracted and executed construction of new customer-oriented facilities to accommodate consolidated organization.

Finance

- Developed higher-yielding investment and pricing strategy for business.
- Grew revenues from $2 million annually to $68-million over 5 years with margins of 2:1.
- Moved funds from low-yielding UK vehicles to higher-performing vehicle recognizing $500 million per year in incremental revenues.
- Established expense-control procedures to manage the business spending.

Business Management

- Acted as sole Spokesperson.
- Managed all legal and regulatory issues with U.S. Regulatory Commissions, Justice Department and external and internal legal staffs.
- Via the creation of tight Business Procedures, eliminated all audit exceptions and delivered 6 years of Passed Audits.
- Merged operations and marketing personnel into one business team.
- Developed technological advances that gave Amrock a clear competitive advantage.
  - Positioned Amrock as the service leader via superior quality and timeliness standards and Zero Defects Discipline . . .
    . . . the only business in the industry with these standards.

Commerical Products Business Manager, contd.

Marketing & Sales

- Developed and managed a <u>Public Relations and Advertising campaign</u> with budget of $1mm.
- Established presence in <u>27 countries</u> from original 10 countries.

  — <u>Called on major prospects and clients 4 times a year</u> to demonstrate Corporate Commitment and close sales (80% travel).

  — <u>Personally raised visibility</u> of Amrock by active involvement in both Amrock-sponsored and Industry seminars, TV and Radio.

- <u>Expanded the corporate client base</u> <u>from 184 clients to 424 ; the Manufacturing Client base from 35 to 80; and the Agricultural Client Base from 10 to 500.</u>

- <u>Established and maintained</u> a client and prospect base of <u>4000 accounts</u>.
  — Including: Hanson, NewsCorp, Hitachi, KLM, WPP, Reuters, ADT, Pirelli, NOL, Keppel, UK Electric, Petrofina, ...

- Creative developer of Quality Marketing and Sales Programs.
  — Developed all collateral materials for the business.
    — Information Packs, Brochures and Sales Aides
    — Direct Mail Campaigns

- <u>Developed Amrock Industry Newsletter</u>, "Info Access" for distribution to 4000 Prospects and Clients; <u>Viewed as industry standard for quality and value added</u>.

Global Manufacturing Marketing Manager   1984 - 1986
Vice President

Introduced "repackaged" global product.
- Developed the strategic and product plans.
- <u>Developed targeted sales and marketing programs</u> to reestablish Amrock presence.
- <u>Turned around major clients' negativism</u> on largest Amrock accounts.
- <u>Staffed organization</u> with industry experts.

Director, Global Product Development
Amrock Services Inc.   1981 - 1984
- <u>Responsible for Development P&L</u>; revenues of $12MM; expense base of $7.5MM over 3 years.
- Developed and delivered <u>marketing support and training programs</u> for domestic sales personnel.
- <u>Created, staffed and managed a regionally based customer-service unit</u> to support sales personnel and to deliver the product.
- Developed multi-currency capability for the U.S. dollar draft product; developed all training and support programs.

AMROCK, INC., contd.

Vice President/*Director of Strategic Planning & Product Development* 1977 - 1981
Consumer Products Group (CPG)

- <u>Developed strategic plan</u> for the Division, a new startup venture.
  — Plan was used as a model for all CPG Divisions.
- Defined the six business ventures and revenue opportunities.

- Developed and then <u>managed the consumer services product area</u>.
- <u>Designed, sold and delivered key consumer products</u> to CEOs:
  - Strategic Planning
  - Consulting
  - Credit Scoring

Human Resource Line Manager 1976 - 1978

- Responsible for direct personnel support to 3 Division Executives plus staff of 1200.
  - Compensation   - Benefits   - Employee Issues   - Counseling

Manager, Combined Management Information Systems 1974 - 1976

- Project Manager for replacement system for automated Head Office General Ledger.

Assistant Manager 1970 - 1974

- As Project Manager, developed and implemented the first Amrock automated telephone information system and company-wide automated directory.
- As Cost and Product Analyst, developed unit costs for branch systems and operations division.

EDUCATION

B.A., University of Honolulu

Executive Management School, University of Chicago

Member UK Securities Association
Marketplace Management
Quality College

ASSOCIATIONS

Member of Chamber of Commerce of France, Japan, Britain and Germany

International Operations Association (IOA)

Financial Women's Association (FWA)

The
Five
O'Clock
Club®

Harold Greenberg:
Getting a Promotion

A person working for the government who wants another government job has to be low-key in stating his accomplishments. He can't brag, for example, about the famous criminals he has captured.

However, the following résumé lists Harold's extensive Certifications and Commendations, which take an entire page, followed by all of his Specialized Training and Courses, which take another page, followed by his education and then outside activities that show he was a good citizen (Cubmaster, etc.). It is easy to see that he has always been an outstanding performer. In addition, Harold thought it was important to include the personal information at the end of his résumé. He had not yet met a number of those who would decide about the promotion. He wanted them to know about his stable family situation, as well as his physical size—given the kind of work he did.

You can see how Harold understated his accomplishments. Do not worry about the résumé length. It was necessary to take this many pages to present the information in a readable way. For example, if he had squeezed his basic career history onto one page, it would have been unreadable. The material was presented on high-quality ivory stock, stapled in the upper left-hand corner. Harold came across as someone who cared—someone who did more, tried to learn more, and was recognized throughout his career.

By the way, Harold's résumé helped him get the major promotion he wanted. There were many competitors for the job, but none had Harold's credentials—and it is safe to assume that no one presented his or her credentials as well as Harold did.

Harold R. Greenberg

15 Haverbrook Drive
Cash-in-Hand, NV 14555

Summary of Qualifications

<u>Career State Investigator</u> having 19 years experience;
over 14 years with the Division of Criminal Justice.

Extended diversified exposure both conducting and supervising investigation into the areas of Economic Crime, Organized Crime, and Official Corruption.

Since 1981, was a Division Instructor and representative to groups interested in the subject of various types of finance-related crime, its detection, investigation, and prosecution.

Professional Experience

Nevada Division of Criminal Justice, 1979-present
Office of the Attorney General

SUPERVISING STATE INVESTIGATOR OF THE   1991-present
ORGANIZED CRIME AND RACKETEERING BUREAU

Conduct both financial and non-financial investigations of allegations concerning Organized Crime and Official Corruption.

Special Prosecutions Section   1986-1991

➢ Assigned to this section to investigate allegations of organized crime and official corruption.

➢ Specialized in financial implications.

➢ Investigations conducted for most part with Nevada State Police and allied agencies.

Major Fraud Unit   1979-1986
   Senior State Investigator
   State Investigator

➢ Conducted primarily finance-related investigations.

➢ Investigations involved areas such as:
   • bank fraud and embezzlements,
   • securities fraud (stocks, bonds, commodities and other invest-
      ment schemes),
   • insurance fraud (including reinsurance fraud),
   • taxation frauds (including income taxation),
   • sales and use tax,

100

Major Fraud Unit, contd.

➤ Areas involved, contd.:

- excise taxes (i.e., motor fuels and employment taxes),
- unemployment fraud conspiracies, and
- other various schemes and offenses.

➤ Conducted investigation on individual and supervisory basis with Division personnel, and with allied governmental agencies as necessary.

Nevada State Law Enforcement Planning Agency-   1976-1979
Executive Office of the Governor

Audit Supervisor
Auditor

➤ Established audit procedures and audit programs.

➤ Conducted audits.

➤ Supervised 5 staff auditors on statewide basis.

Internal Revenue Service, Reno District   1975-1976

Internal Revenue Agent—Field Audit

➤ Conducted audits of individuals, partnerships and corporations as to Federal Income Taxes.

Nevada State Treasury, Division of Taxation   1974-1975
Auditor-Accountant: Field

➤ After college graduation, began as auditor-accountant trainee in corporate tax bureau.
➤ Then assigned as Field Auditor responsible for individual audits of corporations as to state taxes.

CERTIFICATIONS AND COMMENDATIONS

Certified Police Instructor

Since 1981, Division Lecturer on various types of
White-Collar Crime, Organized Crime and Official Corruption.

Specialized presentations on:

- Arson for Profit,
- Money Laundering, and
- Counterfeiting.

Certificate of Commendation
Upperville County Prosecutor's Office

Letter of Commendation
United States Congressman Martin Shulman

Letter of Commendation
Donald O'Connor
1st Assistant Attorney General & Director of Criminal Justice

Letter of Commendation
Dr. Saul Valvanis, Commissioner
Nevada Department of Education

Letter of Commendation
Commissioner Mary Purcello
Nevada Department of Banking

Letters of Commendation from
Various Societies and Organizations

American Bankers Association
Northern and Southern Districts of Nevada

American Society for Industrial Security Officers

Petroleum Security Officers Association

Nevada State University
Accounting Society

Nevada Commission of Investigation (S.C.I.)

Others as to State Employment

Citation: Nevada State Assembly
as to Community work with Scouts as Cubmaster

1993-present
Certified Public Manager Program
Continuing program sponsored by
Nevada Department of Personnel and Reno University.

1993
Roundtable: Money Laundering
Two-day seminar held at Main Treasury Building, Washington, D.C.,
sponsored by U.S. Assistant Secretary of Treasury.

1991
Supervising Undercover Investigations
Four-day course sponsored by the **University of Delaware** concentrating on
covert narcotics and organized-crime investigations.

1986
Racketeer Influenced Corrupt Organization (R.I.C.O.)
Sponsored by Nevada Division of Criminal Justice. 1 week course.
Also participated as Instructor for "Interpreting Financial Statements."

1985
Seminar: White Collar Crime-Investigation and Prosecution
1 week. Battelle Institute, Seattle, Washington
Also participated as Instructor as to utilizing the "Net Worth" approach
as an investigative technique.

1979
Special Agent Training: Intelligence Division, U.S. Treasury
As State Investigator, completed 8-week course at National Training Center
in Washington, D.C., by enrollment in class of Federal Agents. Final two weeks
was Inter-Agency training with Secret Service, Securities & Exchange Commission, F.B.I., and Bureau of Alcohol, Tobacco & Firearms.

Firearms Training and Personal Defense
Police Academy, Upperville County - 2 weeks.

Investigation of White-Collar Crime and Official Corruption
Sponsored by **Seton Hall University** in conjunction with
Peat, Marwick & Mitchell. 2-week course.

1978
Advanced Training for State Auditors
Held at Federal Inter-Agency Training Center, San Diego, CA. 3 weeks.

1976
Basic Training for State Auditors
Held at the Federal Inter-Agency Training Center, San Diego, CA. 3 weeks.

1975
Internal Revenue Agent Training
Held in Philadelphia, PA. This 7-week course included education and
application of Taxation Code, Regs, Cases and Rulings, and audit procedures.

SPECIALIZED TRAINING AND COURSES. contd.

On other various dates received specialized training held at
Division of Criminal Justice such as related to:

- Wiretap and Electronic Surveillance,
- Grand Jury Training,
- Search and Seizure, etc.

EDUCATION

1974	B.S., Commerce, Reno College Major: Business Administration/Accounting
	Post-degree coursework in: Taxation, Investments, and Computers
1981	Passed Nevada State examination for Investment Securities Brokers and Dealers Received principal rating.
current	Certified Public Manager program, in conjunction with Nevada State University Completed two of three sessions.

OUTSIDE ACTIVITIES

Cubmaster - Pack 60
Cub Scouts, Cash-in-Hand, Nevada

Trustee and Treasurer
Robert Jordan Memorial Scholarship Fund

PERSONAL

Married, 3 children
Age - 43
Height - 6'3"
Weight - 218 lbs.

The
Five
O'Clock
Club®

Richard Kunstler:
One Person, Two Résumés

Richard had worked in essentially the same job for well over twenty years. Having opted for early retirement, he considered going in two completely different directions. One was a continuation of his present career in private banking—a field that was very tight. His second option was a lot more fun: he could see himself in an administrative role—for a major foundation or art museum, or even working in a decorating house.

Richard had strong administrative skills, and a wealth of experience in activities outside of his regular job. He served as the treasurer of a not-for-profit organization, and he also served for many years as the president of his cooperative apartment building.

One résumé emphasizes his banking background; the other presents a more rounded person and gives more weight to his extracurricular experiences.

The banking résumé is also an example of functional information presented within a chronological format.

M. RICHARD KUNSTLER

71 South 44th Street
New York, NY 10001

Home: (212) 555-1111
Office: (212) 559-0000

SUMMARY OF QUALIFICATIONS

An administrative manager with broad experience in running operations. In-depth work with accountants, lawyers, agents, and so on. Over 20 years' experience as a trust officer handling all aspects of fiduciary relationships for PremierBank's private banking clients (175 families with overall net worth of $400 million). Expert in all financial arrangements (trust & estate accounts, asset management, non-profit, and tenant shareholder negotiations), as well as real estate matters. Have worked with New York's most prestigious law firms. Extensive experience in staffing.

PROFESSIONAL EXPERIENCE

PREMIERBANK - PRIVATE BANKING DIVISION   1965 - PRESENT

Relationship Manager

Responsible for overall management of 175 family relationships having an overall net worth of $400 million. Coordinated trust, investment advisory, custodial and banking services. Co-ordinate co-trustees, attorneys, account-ants and beneficiaries.

o Saved family $3 million in taxes up front by the use of an innovative estate-planning method.

o Developed a complete estate plan for a family whose financial arrange-ments were in disarray: They had archaic wills and no tax planning in the event of death. Resulted in their having appropriate wills, trusts for children, investment account for wife with gifted securities, and a new attorney and accountant.

o Broad knowledge of discretionary powers, fiduciary accounting, tax appli-cations and investment requirements.

o Reviewed complex financial situations, weighing options vis-a-vis income payments, gifts and estate impact. As liaison between family members, attorney and advisors, formulated annual financial programs saving one client $30,000 annually in taxes.

o As consultant to a wealthy family in jeopardy of losing $600-million income flow and having U.S. assets attached, analyzed all accounts determining precise options available. Evolved a plan through the use of assignments and off-shore corporations to preserve income and assets.

President, 71 SOUTH 44TH STREET CORPORATION INC.   1978 - Present

   o **Run a premiere building - set very high standards.**

   o Closely direct the managing agent and superintendent who oversee a staff of 7 serving a 38-unit apartment building. Resulted in minimum turnover of staff and priority attention from the managing agent.

   o Screen all prospective tenant shareholder applicants as to financial and personal qualifications. Instituted a new way of dealing with applicants that avoided lawsuits while maintaining apartment quality.

   o As President, interface with board of directors on matters of policy, building maintenance, operating expenses and revenues. With Treasurer, chart anticipated capital improvements and budget appropriately.

   o Act as liaison with outside counsel.

   o Recommended and implemented an innovative revenue concept resulting in greater financial security for the corporation.

Treasurer, THE LOGOS SOCIETY OF NEW YORK   1977 - Present

   o **Very much improved the solvency of this organization.**

   o Manage operating budget, and track sources of all revenue and expenditures, both operating and capital improvements.

   o Coordinate in-house and outside accountants. Monitor all legal and financial matters concerning gifts, legacies, and other actions affecting the organization including contracts.

   o Oversee all investments and real estate matters. Sold old headquarters, and recommended the sale of abutting property resulting in financial solvency.

   o Monitor staffing requirements. Put in retired businessman to better run the clinic and allow doctors to serve clients.

   o Individual fund raising resulted in two $100,000-plus legacies.

   o Work with lawyers regarding publishing contracts, leases, and other matters.

EDUCATION

New York University	Graduate Courses: Business Law Accounting, Corporate Management	1962
St. Crispin University	BA, Business Admin./Economics	1964

M. RICHARD KUNSTLER

71 South 44th Street
New York, NY 10001

Office: (212) 559-0000
Office: (212) 555-1111

SUMMARY OF EXPERIENCE

Over 20 years' experience handling all aspects of fiduciary relationships for **PremierBank's private clients: (175 families with overall net worth of $400 million)**. Successfully increased revenue through new business efforts, client cultivation and account assessment. Consistently achieved fee increases resulting in bonus awards. Work well with high-net-worth individuals.

PROFESSIONAL EXPERIENCE

PREMIERBANK - PRIVATE BANKING DIVISION   **1965 - PRESENT**

RELATIONSHIP MANAGER - Private Banking Division   1977 - Present
TRUST OFFICER - Investment Management Group   1970 - 1977

Handle all aspects of fiduciary relationships for PremierBank's private banking clients: 175 families with overall net worth of $400 million.

o As a seasoned account officer, assigned the most difficult, time-consuming accounts that presumably had the lowest potential. Turned the accounts around. Achieved fee increases. Received bonuses.

o Recently gained an $18-million will appointment one week before person's death. Generated $350,000 fee.

o Saved family $3 million in taxes up front by the use of an innovative estate planning method.

o Developed a complete estate plan for a family whose financial arrangements were in disarray: They had archaic wills and no tax planning in the event of death. Resulted in their having appropriate wills, trusts for children, investment account for wife with gifted securities, and a new attorney and accountant.

AREAS OF SPECIAL COMPETENCE

Client Relations

o Identified 50 cases (20% of account base) where client dissatisfaction existed. Established one-on-one contact to identify problem areas. Instituted aggressive service campaigns and quarterly review meetings. Within two years gained confidence of 96% of dissatisfied customers. Obtained $26MM in new business and retained a vulnerable $10-million account.

o Recognized importance of interfacing with several hundred attorneys, accountants and financial advisors. Maintained high profile through constant contact and briefings. Won their esteem. Resulted in a greater working compatibility, efficient decision-making and gaining new business. In one instance, obtained a $60-million account relationship.

108

Consulting

o Reviewed complex financial situations, weighing options vis-a-vis income payments, gifts and estate impact. As liaison between family members, attorney and advisors, formulated annual financial programs saving one client $30 million annually in taxes.

o In capacity as a consultant to a wealthy family in jeopardy of losing $600-million income flow and having U.S. assets attached, analyzed all accounts determining precise options available. Evolved a plan through the use of assignments and off-shore corporations to preserve income and assets.

Analysis and Planning

o Evaluated requests for special payments of capital assets and income. Assessed propriety of payments, researching provisions covering such discretionary actions, consulting with attorneys, family members and accountants. Processed and documented approximately 75 requests annually with 100% of recommendations being accepted.

o Developed improved alternatives to outdated operational procedures. Formulated a new plan for handling over 1500 telephone requests during a 2-month period. Coordinated with Operation Department to establish direct customer wire into central information center eliminating 5000 unnecessary calls. In another instance, developed Form Letters reducing expense in responding by 95%.

o Analyzed 260 accounts for substandard fees. Developed a strategic plan to align revenue with services. Aggressive action and persistence resulted in fee increases adding $200 million to revenues annually.

EDUCATION

New York University	Graduate Courses: Business Law, Accounting, Corporate Management	1967
St. Crispin University	BA, Business Admin./Economics	1964

ASSOCIATIONS

Director of co-operative apartment building   1978 - Present
    President of Board in 1979. Operating budget $650 million.

Director of The Logos Society of New York   1977 - Present
    Served as Vice President. Treasurer in 1978.
    Operating budget $1M.

Philippe Albarello: Aiming at Very Different Targets

*. . .When a man is in turmoil how shall
he find peace
Save by staying patient till the stream
clears?
How can a man's life keep its course
If he will not let it flow?
Those who flow as life flows know
They need no other force:
They feel no wear, They feel no tear,
They need no mending, no repair.*
　　　　　Lao Tzu
　　　　　Translated by Witter Bynner

*We do not succeed in changing things
according to our desire, but gradually our
desire changes. The situation that we hoped
to change because it was intolerable becomes unimportant. We have not managed
to surmount the obstacle, as we were ab-
solutely determined to do, but life has
taken us round it, led us past it, and then
if we turn round to gaze at the remote past,
we can barely catch sight of it, so imper-
ceptible has it become.*
　　　　　Marcel Proust

*I'm very lucky. If it wasn't for golf, I
don't know what I'd be doing. If my IQ
had been two points lower, I'd have been
a plant somewhere.*
　　　　　Lee Travino, as quoted in *Golfweek*

Since he was looking for a job anyway, Philippe thought he might as well explore two targets: one in his current field, purchasing; and one having to do with his passion, sports.

He would need two résumés, since these were such different targets. Many job hunters think they need different résumés for every target they are going after. But usually the fields one person is interested in are not as different as they may seem. For instance, Norman Neumann, whose résumé we saw earlier, had wanted one for the fashion industry and one for a job search outside that industry. In fact, one résumé served both purposes.

Philippe ended up with an excellent position in the purchasing field--one very close to home, and with an increase in salary.

But his exploration of the sports field helped him understand just how important it was in his life. Managing cycling events was central to his family life. His entire family participated in running an annual event, and he was unwilling to give it up. After Philippe negotiated the salary for the new job, he told the hiring manager that he had been an Olympic cyclist, and that he was committed to running the annual cycling event in his town, an undertaking that took two weeks of his and his family's time. Philippe asked if there was any way he could get an extra two weeks off every year to run the event.

The company agreed to the extra time off--with pay—and offered to sponsor the event!

Philippe Albarello

47 Courbet Plaza
Bernini Square, MS 55700

Home: (555) 555-7844
Business: (222) 555-5564

Innovative Purchasing Department Head ($55 million annually) with a high level of integrity and over 15 years at Amdahl. Experience in automation, equipment evaluation, forms management and data processing. Created a divisional Purchasing Department resulting in $4-million savings. Served as Corporate Fleet Administrator (a fleet of 1300) and Contracts Negotiator resulting in savings of $2.4 million.

EXPERIENCE

AMDAHL   1976 - Present

PURCHASING MANAGER   1991 - Present
Amdahl Properties

Supervise staff of 8 in Purchasing and 6 in Payables, $55-million annual volume, 3600 purchase orders processed annually.

- Selected to **create divisional purchasing department** where none previously existed.

    - **Served as the standard for otherAmdahl purchasing departments**.
    - Trained managers to set up other purchasing departments.
    - A professionally-run model operation set up as a profit center, charging for our services.
    - Set up automated purchasing system.
    - Produced a total package of controls to inform management regarding spending.
    - Developed an MIS interface with fixed asset, financial control, and the corporate technology areas.
    - Consistently exceeded goals set by minority/women's vendor program.

- Consistently developed innovative cost-saving methods.

    - **Saved $4 million** through creation of computer and copier lease analysis program.
    - Renegotiated corporate discount on personal computers from 15% to 35%, resulting in **savings of $1 million**.
    - Created a surplus and trade-in program resulting in a **savings of $200,000**.

- Wrote The Purchasing Policy Manual

    - Served as a prototype for other divisions in Amdahl.
    - Evaluated personal computers, desktop publishing, facsimile, microfilm, office and other equipment.

- Preparation of all budget and financial reports.

- Published Purchasing Newsletter for distribution to other purchasing departments, financial controllers, and end users.

SENIOR BUYER   1989 - 1991
AMDAHL Corporate Purchasing Department

- Rated #1 buyer.
- Assisted in the purchase of $50 million annually of computers and related equipment.
- Negotiated national and short-term contracts for corporate and specific needs.
- Served as Corporate Fleet Administrator
  - Fleet of 1330 vehicles.
  - **Saved $2.4 million** through renegotiation of lease.
  - Supervised fleet administrators throughout United States.
  - Developed recommended vehicle list with emphasis on reduced operating costs.
  - Set up Mailroom operation for AMDAHL Delaware.

CITIBANK Corporate Payables Department   1986 - 1988
Senior Operator/Assistant Systems Analyst

- Involved in selection, testing and installation of new equipment.
- Project coordinator for implementation of online purchasing system.
- Served as telecommunications intermediary for in-house and external clients.
- Handled leasing requirements of users.

CITIBANK Corporate Machine Repair   1979 - 1985
Senior Service Technician

- Service full range of microfilm equipment and automated filing systems.
- Supervise equipment warehouse facility for storage and distribution of surplus.
- Renegotiated replacement parts purchase discount resulting in a savings of $300,000.

SPERRY RAND CORPORATION   1974 - 1979

Territorial responsibility for service of complete line of microfilm and automated filing systems.

EDUCATION

AAS Business   City University of New York

Philippe Albarello

47 Courbet Plaza
Bernini Square, MS 55700

Home: (555) 555-7844
Business: (222) 555-5564

SUMMARY OF QUALIFICATIONS

A lifetime involvement in competitive sports – participation, administration and promotion. Ongoing relationships with corporate sponsors and local governments. Personal connections with TV, radio and newspapers to bring events to the public. Work closely with The U.S. Cycling Federation. Manage cycling championships. Won over 100 races including 3rd place <u>1993 Olympic Trials</u>. Former <u>President of MSSC</u>. <u>Annually promote the largest race in the state</u>. Persuasive detail-oriented manager who overcomes obstacles to successfully complete projects.

PARTICIPATION

Extensive athletic background including scholastic involvement in gymnastics, track and karate and amateur-level weight lifting, cycling.

- National Cycling Champion, 1964
- 3rd Place 1984 Olympic Trials - kilometer
- Won over 100 races.

ASSOCIATION POSITIONS HELD

Utilized expertise and personal contacts to successfully organize, develop and present cycling events exhibitions to showcase cycling to business, and potential sponsoring organizations.

President, GBSC

- Secured sponsorship of Windsor bicycles.
- Put together a national-level team including 6 state, national and Olympic winners.
- Oversaw or directed:
  - awards banquet
  - annual racing program
  - 5 races
- Served as media contact.

President and Founder, Missouri Bicycle Club

Formed to promote development of Olympic cyclists in the state.
- Organized the 7-Eleven Missouri Cycling Classics.
  - Worked with sponsors, government, Chamber of Commerce.
  - Directed it for 5 years.
- Brought Olympic-level cycling (featuring Eric Heyden) to Missouri.
- Served as media contact.

Race Chairman, Missouri Wheelman

- Conducted weight lifting and training clinics.
- Directed the Missouri County Cycling Classic.
- Secured sponsorship from bicycle companies.
- Served as media contact.

GOVERNMENT-RELATED EVENTS RUN

Successfully work with governments and government agencies to secure necessary service (police & ambulance), highway sanitation. Coordinate mailings and promotions with government PR people, sports units, Chambers of Commerce. Examples include:

- U.S.C.F.
  - Meet regularly with The District Representative.
  - Meet weekly with The Assistant Executive Director to organize National championships.
  - Arrange housing, food, welcoming reception.

- Eliot County, Dept. of Recreation and Parks
  - Handle every detail. Close contact covering every detail from sign making and banners to securing showmobile platform, hiring the announcer and phototimer.
  - Coordinate publicity and distribute information with Sports Unit.
  - Work with Commissioner to handle logistics.
  - Work with Sponsorship Coordinator to attract sponsors.
  - Missouri Tourism Bureau

- For major events, secure the cooperation of all the governments and agencies involved.

PROMOTE MAJOR EVENTS

- Served as cycling spokesperson for Missouri. A key player.
- 7-Eleven Cycling Classic
  - Initiated and developed this national event.
  - Recruited Eric Heyden and other members of the Olympic Team.
  - Handled all details for 5 years.
  - Served as the media contact.
  - Secured the sponsorship of 7-Eleven.
- Put together programs for events (coordinate typesetters, printers, etc.)
- Interface with all major media: radio, TV and print. Personally know all the reporters and editors.
- Outstanding Citizen Award from Eliot County, 1993.

Other Events Promoted:

Missouri Cycling Classic	Giacometti Dave Cycling Classic
Eliot Country Cycling Classic	1989 Masters National Criterion Championships
Byron Lake	Halloween Cycling Classic

SECURED CORPORATE SPONSORS

7-Eleven	Hewlett-Packard	Nynex
Manchester	Epson	NEC
	Saven	

ALSO HAVE EXTENSIVE CORPORATE EXPERIENCE

Howard Biff: Repositioned for Health Care

You have brains in your head.
You have feet in your shoes.
You can steer yourself
any direction you choose.
You're on your own. And you know what
*   you know.*
And YOU are the guy who'll decide where
*   to go.*
    Dr. Seuss, *Oh, the Places You'll Go!*

Howard had spent his entire working life in banking. Now he needed to look for a job, but banking was retrenching. (In fact, 78 percent of the people who lost their jobs in his bank ended up leaving the banking industry.) Therefore he decided to hedge his bets by targeting banking, as well as a growth industry—health care.

Howard took his bank-operations background, got rid of the jargon, and highlighted those areas that would interest managers in hospitals and other health-care claims processing centers.

In addition, Howard seriously targeted health care by meeting lots of people in the field, joining health-care administration associations, subscribing to health-care trade journals, and networking into lots of hospitals.

The changes in his résumé may seem subtle, but they made all the difference in the world. For example, the term "financial services" is dropped in the headline of the health-care summary. The first bullet on the banking summary lists operational areas specific to banking, while the health-care summary emphasizes generalized transaction processing, with no specifics.

To make it simpler, we have included here only the summaries. The body of each résumé stayed the same.

By the way, Howard ended up in an exciting job in health care.

<u>Summary of Qualifications</u>

Financial Services Operations and Control Executive
with a uniquely strong data processing and systems background;
experienced in turnarounds and conversions.

- Managed **every aspect of operations**: check processing, security processing, lockbox, charge card processing, ATM and POS settlement.

- Controlled every major financial services application: deposit accounting, trust accounting, cash management and electronic funds transfer.

- **Turned around** failing operations. <u>Built</u> management <u>teams</u>.

- Managed **large-scale systems conversions and consolidations**.

- Designed management information and **quality improvement systems**.

- **Assessed entire operations** designing new workflow and control processes.

<u>Areas of Expertise</u>

• Transaction processing management	• Accounting and control
• Workflow analysis	• Team building
• Starting up operations	• Planning/Restructuring

- A participative manager who builds consensus.
- As a senior manager, work effectively with top management and boards.
- Experienced and successful in turning around and starting up operations.
- A strong planner, having successfully managed large system conversions/operation consolidations.

<u>Summary of Qualifications</u>

Operations and Control Executive
with a uniquely strong data processing and systems background;
experienced in turnarounds and conversions.

- Managed numerous **transaction processing** operations, all high volume and computer based.

- **Developed claim tracking systems** and management informations systems that cut costs, reduced risk and improved customer service.

- Led major technical conversions, managing both systems analysts and operations personnel, in multi-million dollar computer projects.

- Implemented accounting and control methods that corrected major financial control problems.

- Assessed entire operations, designing new work flows and control processes.

- **Turned around failing operations** by building management teams and eliminating fundamental problems within the operation.

<u>Areas of Expertise</u>

- Transaction processing management
- Workflow analysis
- Starting up operations

- Accounting and control
- Team building
- Planning/Restructuring

- A participative manager who builds consensus.
- As a senior manager, work effectively with top management and boards.
- Experienced and successful in turning around and starting up operations.
- A strong planner, having successfully managed large system conversions/operation consolidations.

Janet Fudyma: A Lawyer?
Or a Chief Financial Officer?

We act as though comfort and luxury were the chief requirements of life, when all we need to make us happy is something to be enthusiastic about.
Charles Kingsley

Understanding is a wellspring of life to him that hath it.
Proverbs

Janet was tired of telling people that she was more than a lawyer. Her title was Corporate Counsel, but her other responsibilities were more important.

After much probing, we discovered that the ideal next job for Janet would be as Chief Financial and Administrative Officer in a medium-sized firm-- exactly what she was currently doing.

With clients, I sometimes feel like Perry Mason in court. Here is a shortened version of our discussion:

Kate: "Janet, you are having trouble with your job search because you list Corporate Counsel as your job title, and that is how people see you. You keep trying to convince people that you were actually doing something else. But if you call yourself Corporate Counsel on your résumé, you are creating a handicap for yourself."

Janet: "But that was my title, and if people read my résumé very closely, they will see that I also handled all financial and administrative matters for the company."

Kate: "People won't read your résumé very closely. Your résumé is a marketing piece, not a legal document. Could we truthfully say that you were the Chief Financial Officer for the company?"

Janet: "That wasn't my title."

Kate: "Was there anyone else in the company who could have been called the Chief Financial Officer?"

Janet: "No. I was it."

Kate: "If I had called your company and asked for the Chief Financial Officer, who would I have gotten?"

Janet: "You would have gotten me."

Kate: "Then, in fact, you were the company's Chief Financial Officer?"

Janet: "Yes. But that wasn't my title."

Kate: "Can you see that you are misleading the reader when you call yourself Corporate Counsel when you were in fact the company's Chief Financial Officer? And can you see that <u>what we want to put</u>

<u>on your résumé is a job title that honestly reflects the actual job you were doing</u>—rather than some title they happened to give you? And can you also see that you will **not** get a job as a Chief Financial Officer if you insist on describing your function as Corporate Counsel?"

Janet: "I can see that."

Kate: "Is it true that you were responsible for all administrative matters in the company, such as personnel, computers, and so on?"

Janet: "Yes. That's true."

Kate: "Is it also true that you were the Chief Financial as well as the Chief Administrative Officer for the firm, in addition to being Counsel?"

Janet: "That's true."

Kate: "Would it be inaccurate if we listed your job title as Chief Financial and Administrative Officer?"

Janet: "No."

Kate: "**Listing that as your job title would not only be more accurate, but it would also increase your chances of being viewed that way by the reader.** And that would increase your chances of getting another job doing that same thing. So, let's write it up this way and see how you do in your search with this changed positioning."

Janet: "Okay! Let's go for it."

When you do your résumé, think about the kind of job you want next, and then search your background to find things that support the direction you want to take. In Janet's résumé, we played down her legal background, and played up the financial and administrative experiences.

Janet had another problem: she had had a lot of different jobs. You'll notice, at the bottom of page three, how we list four jobs in such a way that the number is deemphasized.

By the way, Janet's résumé is on a 17" X 11" sheet folded so page 1 is on the front, pages 2 and 3 are inside and 4 is on the back.

JANET H. FUDYMA

2 Grove Street
Philadelphia, PA 19109

Office: (215) 554-2345
Home: (215) 556-1234

SUMMARY

Senior-level executive with broad-based management background. Experienced in corporate, legal and financial matters, human resources, strategic planning and regulatory affairs. Strong emphasis on analyzing and exploiting business opportunities and resolving business problems.

EXPERIENCE

CHICO-LAY U.S.A. INC.   **1987-PRESENT**
Vice President/Corporate Counsel

Vice President/Corporate Counsel for $80-million affiliate of leading multi-national food and beverage products company. Corporate officer with primary responsibility for corporate, legal, financial, treasury, human resources and quality control/quality assurance matters.

- Member of Senior management team responsible for establishing brand cost, pricing and promotional strategies.

- Innovated promotion authorization structure resulting in more accurate forecasting and customer profitability analysis while reducing improper deductions.

- Restructured benefits program to tailor coverage to specific needs of work force, thereby increasing employee morale while decreasing overall benefits costs.

- Restructured credit and accounts payable departments, dramatically increasing operating efficiencies and resulting in significant cash-flow benefits.

- Established Quality Control departments and directed implementation of Q.C. processes within production, warehousing and distribution functions, resulted in decreased scrap and costs associated with improper product handling and rotation.

- Successfully defended numerous advertising claims and challenged those of competitors, allowing company to continue aggressive thrust of products comparisons, while forcing competitors to retreat from focal issues of their campaign.

- Significantly curtailed rapidly growing trend toward illegal imports of company products by instituting landmark law suit against grey importers.

- Developed comprehensive emergency product recall procedures designed to ensure rapid and coordinated actions to minimize company losses and maintain consumer brand loyalty.

- Instituted consumer communication program which drastically reduced response time in addressing consumer inquiries, resulting in increased consumer satisfaction and improved relations with customers and brokers.

DAVIS & ASSOCIATES INC.   **1985-1987**
Vice President and Head of Midwest office of Financial and
Management Consulting firm, Engagements included client firms in construction,
manufacturing, service, communication and retail sectors.

- Opened new office in highly competitve environment and successfully established company reputation for quality and professionalism.

JANET FUDYMA

2 Grove Street
Philadelphia, PA 19109
Residence: 215-556-1234
Business: 215-554-2345

SUMMARY OF QUALIFICATIONS

Chief Financial and Chief Administrative Officer
Corporate Counsel

Manage all areas of corporate, financial and legal matters, strategic planning, regulatory affairs, human resources and quality control.

Areas of Expertise include:

- **Overall Business Management**
- **Financing**
- **Financial, Business & Production Controls**
- **Management/Planning/Restructuring**
- **Developing Management Personnel**
- **Strategic Planning**
- **Negotiating Skills**
- **New Business Development**

- Served as CFO for **entrepreneurially-driven $80 million company**.

- Actively involved in all aspects of running company.

- Provide financial and administrative support to high-growth situations:
  - Expert trouble-shooter and problem-solver.
  - Generate operating efficiencies and productivity improvements.

- A **skilled negotiator**: from dealings with vendors and suppliers to complex contracts and legal matters.

- Develop and motivate staff and management team.

- Strong **support to the sales and marketing** functions:
  - With CEO and VP of Operations, established all brand cost, pricing and promotional strategies.
  - Set all marketing, advertising and promotional budgets.
  - Approved all brand and product communication, labeling, copy and packaging.

A business manager who focuses on profits in growth situations.
Strong strategic vision coupled with overall business sense.
Able to translate strategic vision into workable organizational game plan.

Personable, pragmatic and analytical.
A straight-forward, people-person conversant in many disciplines.
Bring order out of chaos.

CHIEF FINANCIAL AND ADMINISTRATIVE OFFICER
CORPORATE COUNSEL
Chico-Lay USA, Incorporated

1987-Present

Member of Senior management team running this $80 million company.

Corporate officer with primary responsibility for all corporate, financial and legal matters, strategic planning, regulatory affairs, human resources and quality control. Actively involved in all aspects of running the company.

- Designed and implemented **system for structuring deals**:
  - Analyzed account profitability.
  - Improved sales forecasting.
  - Reduced improper customer deductions.

- Managed **all financial and administrative areas:**
  - Took credit and A/R departments that were in disarray, and turned them around.
    - **Dramatically improved cash flow.**
    - Significantly **increased operating efficiencies**.
  - Completely **restructured benefits program**.
    - Decreased overall benefit costs.
    - Increased employee morale.

- Established **Quality Control/Quality Assurance** department:
  - **Decreased** manufacturing **costs**.
  - Developed comprehensive **emergency product recall procedures**:
    - To minimize company losses.
    - To maintain consumer brand loyalty.

  - **Managed Consumer Affairs** function:
    - Drastically reduced response time.
    - Improved relations with customers and brokers.

- As **Corporate Counsel**:
  - **Initiated a landmark lawsuit to curtail illegal gray market imports.**
  - **Forced major competitor to retreat** . . .
    . . . from overly aggressive trade advertising.

VICE PRESIDENT and HEAD OF CHICAGO OFFICE   **1985-1987**
    Davis & Associates Incorporated
    (Financial and Management Consulting Firm)

*Engagements included client firms in construction, manufacturing,
service, retail and communications sectors.*

- Opened new office in highly competitive environment.
- Successfully established company reputation for quality and professionalism.
- Arranged and brokered **$40 million in financing and contracts**
  on behalf of clients.
- Developed **innovative compensation system.**
  - Yielded increased productivity and employee morale.
- Served as **chief spokesperson** for company.
  - Appeared on panels, TV and radio.
  - Increased company visibility.
- Designed **programs to win new clients**.
  - Developed and delivered series of seminars.
  - Resulted in **10% increase in client base**.

KODAK/MGM PICTURES   **1983-1985**

*Manager of Financial Analysis—
for nation's largest videotape duplicator.*

- **Trouble-shooter for cost overruns and program delays.**
- **Headed** finance department **group responsible for** financial analysis of **special project.**
- Responsible for **capital appropriation studies** and **customer/product profitability analysis.**
- Directed corporate treasury activities.

Dobbs, Johnson, McLaughlin & Petersen   1981-1982
- **Associate attorney** with law firm specializing in tax-related matters.

Bucks County Health Department   1979-1981
- **Fiscal Officer** with primary responsibility for all financial and budgetary matters.

Burke Enterprises Incorporated   1974-1979
- **Controller** for chain of restaurants and night clubs.

EDUCATION

Kellogg Graduate School of Management, Northwestern University, 1986-1987
J.D., Thomas M. Cooley Law School, 1980
M.B.A., (Management), Central Michigan University, 1977
B.S. (Accounting), Penn State University, 1974

PROFESSIONAL LICENSES

Admitted to Bar:

State of Pennsylvania - February, 1981
State of Illinois - December, 1981

PROFESSIONAL AFFILIATIONS

Planning Forum
American Bar Association
Pennsylvania State Bar Association
American Corporate Counsel Association

For Junior-Level Employees:
A Summary Makes the Difference

Cecilia is four years out of school; Lillian is a young secretary. In both cases, a summary statement differentiates them from their competitors. Even recent graduates should have a summary--to separate them from all of the other job hunters just out of school.

All résumés--no matter what a person's level is--can include personality traits. It's not enough to know that you have done certain things, it is also relevant to know *how* you did them. Are you especially organized, discreet, innovative? Let the reader know, because your personality is one of the most important things you have to offer.

You will notice that every résumé in this book--even that of the most senior executive--contains personality traits so the reader will get a feeling for the way that person operates.

Cecilia Dobbs

499 East Lancaster Avenue
Wayne, PA 19063

(215) 555-1765 (residence)
(215) 555-8024 (office)

Summary of Qualifications

An honors degree in Marketing (<u>magna cum laude</u>) is coupled with <u>four years of professional marketing experience</u> and a solid history of <u>successful projects, promotions and awards</u>. Ability to coordinate the efforts of many to meet organizational goals. High in energy with strong interpersonal skills.

Professional Skills

Hands-on experience within Marketing includes: Market Research, Marketing Support, Project Management, Public Speaking, Training, Computers and Vendor relations.

Staris Information Services Company   1990 to Present

<u>Marketing Analyst</u>

Supported Product Managers by designing and implementing a variety of projects. Results achieved in this position include:

- Developed contracts, visited branch offices, and gave presentations to sales personnel and management.

- Prepared <u>special reports such as the "Analysis of Commercial Revenue"</u> and "Guide to Writing a Proposal."

- Awarded Marketing's "<u>Outstanding Performer</u> of the Month, " July, 1991. Received for creatively organizing over 300 pages of material for sales manuals at significant cost savings, ahead of schedule and within one month's time.

- <u>Developed and implemented</u> the <u>contracting system</u> for our division. Made presentations <u>instructing the field</u> on the system's processes. Project in line with goal to reopen channel between marketing and sales force.

- <u>Designed Product Blue Book</u>, a handy marketing guide to our products for sales personnel.

- <u>Restructured Marketing Guide</u> to be marketing oriented; previously a marketing policy and procedure manual.

- <u>Created profile questionnaire for Competitive Information System</u>.

- <u>Managed</u> the <u>computerized distribution</u> of several marketing manuals and controlled the content of each.

Bringhan Advertising, Inc.   1989 to 1990

<u>Project Director</u>

Responsible for directing research project of agency clients in the consumer package goods field. Results achieved in this position include:

- <u>Employed various quantitative and qualitative methods</u> for concept tests, taste tests and pre and post advertising tests.
- Met critical deadline three weeks after hire, one week ahead of schedule.
- Involved in all phases of studies from <u>basic design to client presentation.</u>
- Researched and prepared special report on Solar Energy Marketplace.
- Developed strong relations with several research suppliers.

Hilton Research Services 1987 to 1989
Study Director

- Coordinated all production elements for a variety of market research studies including: questionnaire construction and pre-testing, sampling, interviewing, editing and coding, tabulation, assisting in report writing
- Supervised the work of 50 people in a research project for a large data processing client. Consisted of 20,000 interviews conducted via CRT's. Resulted in significant change to client's market strategy.
- Advised study directors on design of of-line research studies.

Survey Programmer II
Assisted programmers in developing electronic questionnaires for the CRT. Maintained survey data and verified tabulated research results.

- Received three promotions within 11 months of hire.

B. M. Smith & Associates Summer Practicum 1989
Study Coordinator
Responsible for conducting a research project to determine most effective type of renovation of client's shopping center. Duties included: sample and questionnaire design, collection of primary and secondary data, tabulation, interpretive analysis of data.

Marymount College of Virginia September, 1986 to May, 1987
Study Skills Instructor
Taught study, presentation and interpersonal skills in 15-week courses to students with academic and personal problems.

Chilton Research Services November, 1983 to August, 1984
Interviewer
Conducted telephone interviews for both consumer and industrial studies. Exceeded quota 100% of the time.

EDUCATION

B.A., magna cum laude, Business Administration, Marymount College of Virginia, 1987
A.A., Business Administration/General Merchandising, Marymount College of Virginia, 1986

Honors and Awards:

- Selected twice for "Who's Who in American Universities."
- Vice President of Student Faculty Council for two successive years.
- Member of four honor societies

CONTINUING EDUCATION

Attended various American Marketing Association seminars on Market Research techniques, as well as courses on Written Communication.

OUTSIDE ACTIVITIES

Television, Radio and Advertising Club (TRAC)
Designed and conducted 1990 membership study.

Network of Women in Computer Technology (NWCT)
Designed and conducted 1991 membership study.

LILLIAN LOWANS
43 Marlborough Lane
North Orange, New Jersey 07999
(908) 555-1111

Summary of Qualifications

 Four years of executive secretarial experience coupled with continuing college education. A solid history of excellent work relationships, both with the public and with internal personnel at all organizational levels. High in initiative and energy with strong ability to exercise independent judgment. Excellent writing skills. Trustworthy and discreet.

Professional Experience

Typing Speed: 75-80 wpm   Shorthand Speed: 95-100 wpm
Qualified to operate all standard business equipment, including word processsors

But more importantly, can take on major projects and handle from initiation and planning through to implementation and follow-up.

Employment History

DataPro   1990 to Present
Senior Secretary to Manager of Pricing Department

Performed general secretarial duties with minimum supervision.

- Represent manager in collecting activity reports from departmental professional staff; compile and draft final report for signature.

- Compose letters independently or from general direction as required.

- Administer the entire Competitive Information System from receipt of information through acknowledgement, analysis flow, publicity, and final entry into the computer system.

- Maintain and monitor correspondence/communication follow-up system.

- Monitor Status of departmental projects.

- Supervise temporary typists.

Intercounty Savings Association   1988 to 1990
Executive Secretary to President

Performed general secretarial/administrative duties and coordinated all personal and business affairs of the President.

- Acted as liaison between President and branch offices, as well as service corporations, the general public, insurance companies, government agencies and members of the U. S. Senate and Congress.

- Calculated daily subsidiary figures to allow determination of funds flow. Based on the outcome, wired and borrowed funds.

- Prepared minutes for Board of Directors and Committee meetings.

- Solicited bids and handled insurance for Association and personnel to comply with Federal guidelines. Maintained approximately 100 personnel records.

- Distributed and administered travelers checks and U.S. Government savings bonds for all branches.

Yarway Corporation   **1985 to 1988**
Secretary to Manager of Manufacturing/Plant Engineering   1986 to 1988

Performed a variety of secretarial duties with little supervision.

- Directed the work flow through the department and supervised a full-time clerk.

- Collected, analyzed and assembled data from reports and print-outs into meaningful logs and charts for manager's use.

- Coordinated the flow of blueprint adaptations to obtain bids for the manufacturing of special tooling.

- Handled a variety of projects at the request of manager.

Assistant to Secretary of Vice President of Manufacturing and   June, 1985 to May, 1986
President of Yarway North American Division

Typed large volumes of correspondence and reports in a timely fashion; Distributed reports; Updated manuals, including Quality Assurance Manual for the ASME; Performed general clerical duties.

Cost Accounting Clerk (part time, work/study program)   September, 1975 to June, 1975

Analyzed routings to determine individual costs of labor and material; Posted figures; and Assisted other members of the Accounting Department in routing accounting functions.

EDUCATION

Plymouth Whitemarsh Senior High School, Whitemarsh, PA
Graduated Class of 1985. Business Major, Work/Study Program

SUPPLEMENTAL EDUCATION (Most recent)

Basic Principles of Supervisory Management Work Organization and Time Management
Improving Management Skills of Secretaries
TSO
Data Preparation

Various Résumés for Professionals and Executives

They can have anything they want, but they can't have everything they want. There is more to life than Kansas. The key is choosing what we want most (our heart's desire), letting go of everything else we want (for now), and moving (mentally, emotionally and physically) toward our goal.

John-Roger and Peter McWilliams,
Do It! Let's Get Off Our Buts

". . . sir, I would like to become a psychologist, but it requires so much training that I'm afraid I would be too old when I finish."

The wise man sat in silence for a few moments, smiled, and then asked, "Young lady, how long would it take you to become a psychologist?"

"About seven years," she replied.

"How old would you be then?" was the next question.

"I will be twenty-five."

Then the man asked, "How old will you be in seven years if you don't become a psychologist?"

Of course, her answer was the same. "Well, I guess I would be about twenty-five."

Time waits for no one. . . . Remember, your future is exactly what you make it.

Dennis Kimbro,
Think and Grow Rich: A Black Choice

On the following pages are additional résumés for people of various levels. In each case, the person thought about his or her target area, and positioned his or her background to fit the target.

Now, take a crack at your own résumé. Then test it with friends. Ask them, "When you look at this résumé, how do I come across?"

The danger here is that when you ask people for comments, they give you comments. Some are worthwhile, some are not. Pay attention to the remarks that have to do with the way you are positioned on your résumé. If you intend to come across as someone who manages people, but the reader sees you as a person who has written press releases, that's a problem that's worth paying attention to. On the other hand, be aware that some people will suggest word changes that are different but not necessarily better.

Incorporate any valuable suggestions and polish up your résumé. Now you're ready to hit your target area.

Archibald Alexander
25 Campanas Street
Santa Fe, NM 87555
505-555-6281

SUMMARY OF QUALIFICATIONS

14 years experience in design and administration in **all areas of employee benefit plans**, including 5 years with **Briar Consultants**. Advised some of the largest and most prestigious companies in the country. Excellent training and communications skills. MBA in Finance. **An effective manager who delivers consistent results**.

NYNAX CORPORATION   1985 - Present
Manager, Stock Plans Administration

Manage an 8-person unit administering Employee Stock Purchase and Executive Stock Option plans.

- o Personal contact with the **4,000 most senior executives**.
- o Accounting and record keeping for **$178 million** in plan assets.
- o **Reduced expenses 25%** through automation and productivity enhancements.
- o Successfully conducted major Stock Purchase plan offering on tight schedule; the largest the company had ever undertaken: **90 countries**; data from 16 payroll systems; distribution of personalized packages to 60,000 employees.
- o Implemented state-of-the-art transaction confirmations system.

BANKERS FIRST COMPANY   1984 - 1985
Defined Contribution Plans Manager

Managed unit of six; **$750 million in plan assets**; 25 client plans.

- o Managed all record keeping, trust and administrative services for very large corporate clients' Savings, 401(K) and Stock Ownership plans.
- o Handled all regulatory and ERISA compliance, cash and securities management, consulting, trust administration and accounting.
- o **Reduced overtime 50%; computer usage 25%; expenses 33%**.

BRIAR CONSULTANTS   1979 - 1984
Defined Contributions Plans Consultant

Managed a unit of 10 consulting on **all phases** of design, implementation and administration of Fortune 500 company plans.

- o **Increased profits 170%**.
- o Handled 25 accounts worth $3.2 million in annual revenue.
- o Managed plan, systems and database design.
- o Supervised system conversions and daily production.
- o Performed market analysis.
- o Delivered sales presentations.
- o Negotiated contracts and fees.
- o Designed reports, statements and administrative forms.

BRIAR CONSULTANTS, INC. (Cont'd)
Defined Benefit Plans Manager

o   Consulted on pension plan design and interpretation, governmental reporting and compliance, record keeping, administrative practices and procedures and the development and use of compliance manuals.

o   Introduced Standardized administration manuals and paperwork reduction techniques which **generated more than $1.2 million in consulting revenue**.

ROYAL INSURANCE COMPANY   1978 - 1979
Assistant Manager, Employee Benefits

o   Compliance Officer.
o   Administered the company's pension, health and other employee benefit plans.
o   Performed medical plan cost containment study and implemented changes resulting in a leveling of insurance premiums.
o   Offered and implemented HMO's.
o   Negotiated insurance contracts with carriers.
o   Performed statistical compensation analysis.

NATIONAL BULK CARRIERS   1978
Employee Benefits Manager

Administered domestic and overseas pension and group medical, life, disability and worker's compensation insurance plans. **Secretary Pension and Employee Benefits Committees**.

STANDARD BRANDS INCORPORATED (now RJR Nabisco)   1975 - 1978
Assistant Pension Supervisor

Administered 12 domestic pension plans covering 23,000 bargaining and non-bargaining employees.

EDUCATION

MBA, Economics and Finance, June 1982
B.A., Psychology, June 1973
ST. JOHN'S UNIVERSITY

Helen Louise Dobbs

44 Cliff Lake Town
Clarksville, New York 10001
Business: 914-555-2550
Residence: 914-555-4557

Summary of Qualifications

8 years' executive experience managing facilities and support services.
Managed and developed **9 service departments** with a **staff of 120**. Reorganized and set quality standards to reduce costs and lower turnover. Implemented training programs, improved morale and the respect of workers for each other. Strong negotiation skills. Work with high technology applications. In a building of 50,000 sq. ft., responsible for **office planning, telecommunications, maintenance, record retention** and company promotion.

Professional Experience

VICE PRESIDENT, OPERATIONS & SUPPORT SERVICES   1981-present
THE KELLOGG GROUP (A subsidiary of Time, Inc.)

Manage a **staff of 120** in **9 service departments**.
Responsible for all **facilities management** for a **50,000 sq. ft. office**.
Manage a budget of **$7-10 million**.
Report directly to the Chairman.

Budgeting, Management and Cost Control
- Manage internal costs. Regularly renegotiate and monitor contracts to **keep costs down**.
- Conduct special analyses and cost comparisons, and purchase research.
- Regularly develop innovative solutions that cut costs in both the short- and long-term.
- Control work overflow resulting in a **smooth-running operation** with rare complaints.
- Set up **system to handle bottlenecks and crisis deadlines**.

Telephones
- Select and maintain a system of **300 phones**: **central to this telemarketing business.**
- Establish special relationships with MCI, WATS, FAX , TELEX.
  - Allows for **special testing**, such as the 96 local lines that were installed for a 3-week test period and removed.
- Developed **a system that never goes down**.

Construction and Maintenance
- Regularly manage demolition and construction of space ranging from 3,000- 7,000 sq. ft.
- Handle all city filings, HVAC regulations, fire alarm systems.
- Handle all design and decoration including carpets, furniture, lighting, wall coverings.
- Maintain 50,000 sq. ft.: floors, walls, and so on.
- Negotiate/maintain cleaning contracts, & maintenance contracts for business machines.

Records Retention
Manage the storage of **30,000 sq. ft. of records.**
- Established a successful **system for quick recall and timely destruction.**
- **Cut storage costs by two-thirds.**

136

VICE PRESIDENT, OPERATIONS & SUPPORT SERVICES, contd.

Printing and Mailings
- Coordinate writing, approval process, and actual printing:
  - company brochures,
  - redesign of company logo,
  - annual Christmas card (designed by kids at Ronald McDonald House).
- Maintain company mailing list. Produce mailings, brochures and self-promotional materials.
- Monitor **high volume, complex, on-deadline outside printing**.

Research Production Department
- **Handle 56 million copies/year.**
- Set up staff to monitor work flow and productivity of research projects as they pass through various areas of the company.
- Monitor project from proposal letter, questionnaire development, word processing, production, distribution and return, validation checking, coding, keypunching, data processing and final report.

Data Processing
- Staff of 10.
- Develop programs for customized research studies.
- UNIX system.
- Maintain 13 remote PC's that are tied in to the UNIX.

N.Y. State Society of CPS's   1979-1981
Office Manager

- Staff of 10.
- Supervised equipment and production requirements to ensure progressive departmental growth.
- Supported three organizational divisions.

NU Financial Aid Department   1974-1979
Assistant to Loan Officer

Advanced Education

Various technical and managerial courses.

Mary J. Grossman

7709-43 Byewell Way
Chicago, IL 99999
312-555-1212

Summary of Qualifications

13 years' experience in retail.
Travel and research of Europe, India and Orient markets. Developed **private label** from initial concept to **bottom line** performance in stores. Strong **financial seasonal planning**. Skilled **negotiator**. **Decision-maker** responding to ever-changing sales and fashion trends. **Catalyst** providing counsel for **teamwork** within divisions.

Professional Experience

DIRECTOR OF SALES AND MARKETING   1989-present
Mary Michael Dress Company
- **Developed sales concept for Mary Michael line.**
  - **Resulted in a dramatic sales increase.**
- **Developed line** from initial concept to finished product.
- Initiated **advertising programs aimed at key accounts**.
- Key account executive.
- Served as liaison between retailer and manufacturer to increase profits for both.

PRODUCT DEVELOPER/BUYER   1988-1989
Dobson, Inc. (16 Plus: 300 large-size specialty stores)
- **Regularly conducted primary consumer research** that resulted in a better understanding of consumer needs and a more appropriate product line.
- **Designed traditional sportswear from initial concept to bottom-line store performance.**
- **Volume 30 million.**
- Developed **financial seasonal** plans.
- Implemented store presentations to coordinate with the total store.

Product Developer/Buyer   1985-1987
MONTGOMERY WARD

- **Created a private-label business in bodywear.**
  - **Business grew from zero to 2 million dollars annually.**
  - **Markup increased from 55% to 60%.**
  - **Turnover increased from 2.5 to 3.0.**
- **Increased volume and market share to establish the company as a serious competitior in my product market.**
- Developed all the **private-label** items for bodywear, casual/sheer hosiery and slippers in domestic and foreign markets.
- Volume 20 million.
- **Seasonal plans** for all categories.
- Communications with field managers to effect profitable operations direct to stores.
- Implemented **brand labels** for department.
- Trained and directed development of both an associate and assistant buyer.

PRODUCT DEVELOPER   1984-1985
J.C.PENNEY & COMPANY

- **Increased India/Orient placements by 75%.**
- **Developed European market research and placements.**
- Researcher of markets in Europe/India/Europe (Jr. moderate/better women's & better separates.)
- Initiated items to divisions for **volume merchandising** in private label/foreign markets.
- Developed **domestic corporate programs** to make divisions proficient and profitable as a total unit with domestic resources.

Buyer/Assistant Buyer   1981-1984
BAMBERGER'S

- **Trained and developed new buyer to comprehend the Jr. market.**
- Seasonal goals.
- Purchases.
- Merchandising stores.
- Effective teamwork with individual store units to **achieve maximum volume** with the merchandise.
- Equal partner with the buyer in planning Jr.-related separates and swimwear.

Buyer   1975-1981
MAYSON'S

- **Developed better Jr. dress business.**
- **Increased volume by 15%.**
- Seasonal planning.
- Purchases.
- Merchandising stores.
- Jr. Dresses/Coats/Women's sportswear.

Education

FASHION INSTITUTE OF TECHNOLOGY
AAS, Apparel Design, 1967-1969

Diane C. Harlington

156-18 Shephard Street
Baton Rouge, LA 99414
999-555-4685

Summary of Qualifications

Manager of 3 service departments:
word processing, proofreading & computer graphics.

- **17 years' business experience.**
- **<u>Staff of 25</u> produces <u>highly complex, highly technical, highly accurate</u> work.**
- **Run an independent department.**
- **Create climate that enhances productivity & cooperation.**
- **<u>Turnover rate</u> almost <u>zero</u>.**
- **Ability to motivate people and keep morale up in
    a <u>very high pressure</u> atmosphere.**

Professional Experience

Director of Word Processing   1982 to present
Decisions Sciences, Inc. (Subsidiary of Amrock, Inc.)

Manage 25 operators and a payroll of $600,000
(3 shifts, 10 word-processing machines, 2 IBM-PC's for computer graphics)

- Average 600-700 hours/week.

- Handle work for 45 people.

- Set up process to tightly **<u>monitor quality control</u>** of this highly technical work.

- Monitor priority work to **<u>meet chaotic deadlines</u>**.

- Train all new hires in an intensive training program.

- Developed an atmosphere that keeps **<u>productivity up and turnover down</u>**.

- **<u>Developed quick-reference manual</u>** to speed the work and reduce errors.

- Able to hire high-quality people with **<u>no agency fees</u>**.

- Supervise small department that produces basic computer graphics.

- Maintain constantly changing mailing list of 3000 names.
    Supervise monthly mailings. Streamlined the mailing-list process.

- **<u>Negotiate</u>** maintenance **<u>contracts</u>** for all hardware and software.

Assistant Bookkeeper   1974-1981
Mercantile Stores

- Responsible for all journal entries, cash receipts, check disbursements, expense book records, general ledger, monthly financial statements.
- Served vendors on a daily basis regarding questions pertaining to remittances.

Billing Assistant

- Responsible for all billings pertaining to purchases by the stores.
- Typed checks for vendors on NCR and Burroughs billing machines.

Courtesy Desk - Bookkeeper   1972-1974
Pathmark Stores

- Handled customer complaints.
- Responsible for coupon transfers to food companies.
- Bookkeeper for front end cash registers and daily deposits.

Dr. Carol Jackson

1336 Union Street
Miami, FL 99213
999-555-5803

Summary of Qualifications

20 years' experience in Program Development for universities and agencies.
Managed **projects ranging from $500,000 to $10 million**.
Directed small art museum. **Determined cultural policy for a small country**.
Ed.D. in International Education, University of Massachusetts, Amherst, MA

Areas of Expertise

- **International Education** in developing countries
- **Arts and Museum Administration**
- Securing **grants of $1 to $5 million each**
- Writing, researching and **publishing**
- Teaching English, African and Caribbean Studies, etc.
- Fluent in English and French

Program Development Experience

Institute of Social and Economic Research   1987-1988
University of Trinidad
Research Fellow

- Managed budget of **$1 million** for special project.
- Conducted an analysis of the effects of Senior Comprehensive schooling on the labour market performance of a sample of vocational graduates.
- **Edited 500-page book**.

Director, The National Museum   1985-1987
West Indies

- Designed and managed efforts to secure and maintain **$5 million** in government assistance to support museum's efforts.
- **Ran day-to-day operation of the museum**.
- **Trained 50 volunteers**.
- **Arranged exhibitions, lectures, panel discussions**, etc.

Senior Professional   1982-1985
Ministry of Sport, Culture and Youth Affairs, West Indies

- **Wrote national policies** on culture and youth.
- Identified and evaluated socio-economic trends.
- Advised Minister on strategies for disbursement of **$60-million budget**.

University of Miami Graduate School   1979-1981
and the Puerto Rican Traveling Theater
Coordinator, Performance Education Program for the U.S. Office of Education

- **Administered after-school program** for minority children.
- Annual budget of $500,000 and a client population of 1000.

University of Michigan   1976-1979
Program Specialist

- Coordinator, The Ghana Project
- Part of a **$10-million** five-year institutional development project funded by the U.S. Agency for International Development.

Assistant Director   1970-1976
Central Detroit Model Cities

- Administered the Early Childhood Resource Center, catering to inner-city children.

Teaching Experience

Adjunct Lecturer, Ann Arbor College; Africana and Puerto Rican Studies Dept.	1972-1975
Educational Opportunity Center, Detroit; English, GED program	1974-1976

Adjunct Lecturer

University of Michigan, School of Education	1976-1979
College of Boca Raton, School of New Resources	1980-1982
University of the West Indies, Department of Language and Linguistics	1983-1988

Consultancies

Dept. of Indian & Eskimo Affairs, Gov't of Canada
Caribbean/American Community Services Council Inc., N.Y.C.
Oxum International, Miami, Florida
Creative Arts Center, University of the West Indies
Organisation of American States, Washington, D.C.
U.S. Agency for International Development/Caricom Secretariat

Professional Affiliations

Phi Delta Kappa
Comparative and International Education Society
Caribbean Studies Association
Anti-Apartheid Organisation of Trinidad and Tobago

Publications

- Carol Jackson (1986, **300 pp.**)
The Independence Experience of The West Indies,
I.S.E.R., Trinidad & Tobago

- **The Vision of Black Artists**;
Carol Jackson (1983)
The Center for African American Art

In Progress:
- Caribbean Contemporary Art
- Focus on Southern Africa

Wilma Albrecht

806 Riverside Estates Road
Altus, N.C. 99712
999-555-9873

Summary of Qualifications

Ten years' freelance experience in writing, editing and proofreading.
Have **edited the writing of at least 45 people**. Backed by 4 years' experience teaching English. Keep balance between respect for the writer's art and the standards set by the organization. Accomplish tasks/goals in an organized, efficient manner with an attitude of pride, sensitivity and self-discipline. Adhere to stylistic standards. B.A. in English.

Professional Experience

Mail Order Manager, Still Pond, Inc.   Jan.-Nov., 1994
Received/processed orders; set up/maintained filing system; corresponded with customers.

Internationally Recognized Not-for-Profit Organization   1979 to 1992
Organization focuses on improving communication techniques, especially in the areas of marriage and family living.

- **Managed a program of 14 presentations a week.**
  - Wrote and delivered 6 different presentations each weekend to groups of 45 people.
  - Edited 8 other presentations each week for 9 years.
  - Critiqued, proofread and **edited the writings of at least 45 other presenters.**
  - Known for thorough, accurate and creative work.
  - Regularly met countless deadlines in both writing and critiquing/editing.

- **Edited bi-monthly newsletter.**
  - Wrote articles for every issue.

- **Co-Director of Operations**, Western North Carolina (1984-1986)
  - Coordinated and gave **final approval of all writing assignments**.
  - Responsible for hiring and firing, budgets and finances.
  - Maintained a balance:
    - sensitivity/respect towards writers and their work,
    - a focus on the final "product" and **meeting standards set by the organizations**,
    - the needs of seminar attendants.
  - **Edited** the organization's **new brochure** (1985).

Altus Elementary School, Parent Volunteer   1979-1988
- Assisted teachers with **proofreading/grading students' creative writing assignments.**
- **Coordinated/edited newspapers** for two class groups.

Teacher, English and Reading   1971-1975
Altus School System, primarily 7th and 8th grades
Focused on grammar/punctuation rules and an appreciation for creative writing and literature.

Education

B.A., English, Altus College, Altus, N.C., 1971
- 3.6 G.P.A. in the 16 English courses taken
- Nominated for Woodrow Wilson Fellowship (1971)
- **Literary Editor** for college yearbook (1970-1971)

M. E. Mullinnix

100 Suttle Road
Springfield, AZ 99764
999-555-4166

Summary of Qualifications
Over 12 years' promotion, sales and managerial experience.
Have trained hundreds of sales people; co-ordinated 1300 distributors. Held 2-3 day seminars. Troubleshooter for sales and distribution problems. An excellent manager and motivator of people. Hold special events that increase business. Strong writing skills including film scripts and advertising copy. An independent and dedicated manager. Sincere, caring & harmonious.

Professional Experience

Founder and General Manager, Interstate Direct Mail   1983-1993
- Founded and ran this company. • Hired six people. • Purchased all equipment.
- Trained and supervised all staff. • Monitored scheduling and deadlines.
- Initiated and followed-up sales calls. • Edited all copy.

Account Sales Executive, KASH AM & FM Radio and KLUC Radio   1981-1983
- At KASH, **specialized in retrieving accounts the company had already lost.**
  - Retrieved 15 accounts.
- Developed **new accounts through** an extremely successful innovative networking approach called a **TIPS CLUB**.

Gift Consultant, Miller & Paine Department Store   1980-1981
Promoted bridal registry through personal letters, phone calls and advertising. Developed innovative idea of visiting Home Ec classes in local high schools.

Regional Sales Manager, Pure Water, Inc.   1977-1979
- Responsible for distributor **sales volume increase in nine-state area**.
  - Educated, motivated and made company decisions to help promote sales.
  - **Increased sales in nine states by one-third the first year.**
  - Doubled distributor sales volume in Florida in one year.
  - **Top salesperson, 1979**.
- Coordinated the **sales of 1000-1300 distributors**.
  - **Trained hundreds of sales people** in 2-3 day meetings.
  - **Taught service people** how to service the machines.
  - Served as a **troubleshooter for** the **sales problems** of all 1300 distributors.
- **Elected M/C at National Conference** working with guest speaker, Zig Zigler.
- Wrote many promotional-selling articles for company magazine.
- Awarded **Regional Manager of the Year** for distributor's sales.

Sales Promotion Manager, Southern Paper Company   1973-1975
Developed new position for increasing sales through an innovative approach:
- Trained prospective customers in how to specify different inks/paper types.
- Held 3-day paper seminars for seven distinct groups.
- Held special events.
- Worked in printing equipment trade shows, local and cooperative state shows.
- Increased sales enough to add two more sales people.

Copywriter/Announcer, KNOT-TV & FM Station   1972-1973
- Wrote TV and FM radio copy.
- Did video TV spots and radio spots.
- Coordinated and directed background scenery. Went on location advising studio photographer for special shots.
- Did a pre-recorded nighttime radio music show.

Editor/Public Relations Manager, Outboard Marine Corp.   1968-1969
- Edited company magazine and handled company P.R. duties.
- Obtained publicity through most national trade magazines.
- Coordinated freelance artists and writers around the country in producing special on-the-spot application stories about the company's products.
- Distributed innovative ideas and encouragement/promotional letters to dealers.
- Attended meetings and conventions.
- Assisted in advertising campaigns, such as photography of products.

Columnist/Sales, Sun Newspapers   1967-1968
- Wrote weekly column.
- Initiated the column and sold ad space.

Copywriter, National Research Bureau   1966-1967
- Wrote ads and idea copy for radio and TV.
- Developed exciting and challenging department-store promotion ideas.

Free-Lance Experience

- Wrote script for the Chamber of Commerce 1972 National film.
- Coordinated and narrated a 1-hour televised live fashion show held in a large private club.
- Participated in voice spots for radio commercials for 3 different stations.
- PR, marketing and advertising for a designer fashion store.

Memberships

Community
- Board Member, Springside Chamber of Commerce, Advertising Committee
- Board Member, Red Cross, Springside
- Board Member, YWCA, Springside

Professional
- Member, Ad Club (2-1/2 years)
- First Vice President, Cornhusker Editor's Association/International Association of Business Communicators
- Promotional/Advertising Manager, Springside Community Players
  - Developed advertising brochure. • Promoted group through tents, brochures, posters.
  - Increased ticket sales by 14%.

Advanced Education

Courses in:

• Advertising	• Journalism	• Magazine editing
• Career Management	• Telemarketing	• Advertising Promotion

Hovsep Jedjizian
753 Mulbury Lane
Minneapolis, Minnesota 99999
222-555-9466

INVESTMENT MANAGER

Senior Officer of $25-billion Investment Management firm

Proven record of successful investment performance:
Senior Fixed Income Portfolio Manager with **top quartile numbers for 8 years**.

Strong relationships with clients:

• Major corporate   • Major Fortune 500 corporate pension funds   • Major not-for-profit institutions

Create, structure and market new products:
Grew department from $1 billion to $3 billion in 6 years.

Board of Directors, Treasurer, Chairman of Investment Committee,
Member of Executive Committee, United Way of Minnesota, 1988 to present

A strong producing manager who is demanding but reasonable and easy to deal with.
Sets high standards of customer service, integrity and professionalism.
Do well in tough environments.

SYNERGY CAPITAL MANAGEMENT   1979-present

SENIOR VICE PRESIDENT (1979-present)
Manager, Fixed Income Department (1979-1985)
Senior Fixed Income Portfolio Manager (1985-present)

Grew department from $1 billion to $3 billion in 6 years.

• Created, structured and marketed new products:
  • Chairman, Synergy Mortgage Securities Income Fund
  • Chairman and President, Synergy Bond Fund
  • President, Synergy Tax-Exempt Fund
  • Senior Vice President, All remaining Synergy Fixed Income Funds

• Turned around the fixed income department. Made it into a first-rate organization.
  • Quickly turned investment results around:
        . . . Went from 4th Quartile in 1979 to 1st Quartile by 1985.
  • Personally managed the largest pension funds and produced 1st Quartile performance.

• Restructured the entire department.
  • Established an investment approach and winning strategy.
  • Convinced the plan sponsors that Synergy Fixed Income had changed.
  • Dramatically improved department morale.

• Diversified the assets:
  • New accounts were a mix of pension, endowment and mutual funds.
  • Created, marketed and managed fixed income products, including open and closed-
    end mutual funds and specialized products for pension funds.

147

General Re CAPITAL MANAGEMENT, Philadelphia, PA   1978-1979

Senior Vice President and Director, Manager of Fixed Income Department

INSTITUTIONAL SALESMAN AND SALES MANAGER   1955-1978
    Various investment dealers

UNITED STATES MILITARY INTELLIGENCE, Washington. D.C.   1956-1958

CURRENT COMMUNITY INVOLVEMENT

UNITED WAY   1988-present

Member, Board of Directors
Treasurer
Chairman of Investment Committee
Member, Executive Committee

- Redefined the investment objectives of the organization.
- A key force in helping to reestablish financial awareness in the association. Now fiscally sound.
- Introduced concepts to allow more secure funding for research grants.

EDUCATION

B.S., Economics, NorthWestern University, 1955

Personal and client references and record of investment performance
from 1982 to 1989 available upon request.

The
Five
O'Clock
Club

Résumés for People with "Nothing To Offer"

Recent college graduates, housewives, or those with very little or very low-level work experience often feel as though they have nothing to offer. They say: "Kate, if I had the experience the people in your examples had, I'd have no trouble writing a résumé."

These people are wrong in a number of ways:

1. Even the highest-level executives have a great deal of difficulty figuring out what their accomplishments have been and preparing their own résumés. Résumé preparation is a skill just as marketing or finance is a skill, and it is not something executives have to do every day on their jobs.

2. You are not competing with high-powered executives. Therefore, it doesn't matter that you haven't run a division of 600 people. If you had run that division, you'd have other problems in preparing your résumé.

3. It's better for each of us, no matter what our experiences, to think that we have done okay considering where we came from. Our experiences have made us what we are today, and that's not so bad. We should be proud of whoever we are, and make the most of it. We should each strive—executive, young person, homemaker—to uncover our special gifts and contributions, and let the world know.

On a national TV program, I was once asked to take an "ordinary housewife" and develop a résumé for her. It was promoted as something akin to magic. Can Kate make this nothing into a something? The producers picked someone who had been at home for twenty years. That would be a good one! Without even seeing her (which increased the illusion of magic), I interviewed the woman and developed a great résumé for her.

Afterwards, the people who worked in the studio said it wasn't fair: we should have picked someone who *really* had nothing to offer. They

were convinced that a typical "ordinary housewife" could not possibly have an interesting résumé. These studio executives were voicing a prejudice that reinforces the way many people feel about themselves.

Of course, in real life, most homemakers are not sitting home doing nothing for twenty years. A career counselor can help find the things anyone has to offer. Every homemaker and every young person has *done things*. With an open mind and the right help, these can be well presented in a résumé.

The Process

Prior to show time, I spent one hour on the phone with Maria, with no preparation on her part. You, however, would be wise to prepare by doing some of the exercises listed below. If you have trouble doing them, don't worry. You can do them with your counselor.

1. <u>List the fields you think you would like to go into</u>. If you have a clear idea about what you want to do in the future, that's great. Even if you don't, you can still have a fine résumé.

2. <u>List all the work you have ever done</u> before your marriage (or school) or during it. It does not matter whether you earned money doing this work. For example, Maria "helped out" in her daughter's store. She didn't get paid for it, but it added a lot to her résumé.

3. <u>List all the volunteer work you have ever done</u>--for your place of worship, school, neighbors and friends. What are the things you find yourself doing again and again? For example, do you find you are always baking cakes for parties, baby-sitting or volunteering to tutor? List these things.

Do not be too timid and squeamish about your actions.
All life is an experiment.
Ralph Waldo Emerson

4. **List any organizations you have belonged to and any courses you have taken.**

5. **List your most important personality traits**. Are your detail-oriented? Are you able to motivate others? Do you follow through on everything you tackle?

6. **List your favorite hobbies, pastimes or interests**. Perhaps, for example, you enjoy needlepoint. I had one client whose passion was bowling--she not only bowled, but she also scheduled tournaments. We were able to make a résumé out of it, and she got a job with a bowling association!

Try to list everything, no matter how silly it seems. Then **set up an appointment with your counselor**.

These are essentially the same exercises top executives do. Again, the Seven Stories Exercise is the key to uncovering those things you enjoyed doing and also did well--and would like to do again. And the exercise is helpful in uncovering other things as well. Through the exercise, you will find out:

• what you have done that you are proud of. In the sample résumés that follow, each person has found something to be proud of, whether it's earning money to go through school or helping a daughter in her shop.

• personality traits that will separate you from the competition, such as the ones noted in the summary statement of Larry's résumé:

productive, self-motivated, and so on.

• how to look at your work, school and volunteer experience objectively. In Larry's example, he spent a great deal of time analyzing the job he had. This analysis gave his résumé a lot of substance.

Even young people with no "real" work experience, or housewives who have been out of the workforce a long while can develop strong résumés—if they can think about their experiences objectively.

And, as with executives, the experiences have to be "repositioned" to fit the target market. For example, Maria said she had helped her daughter in the store. The fact is, Maria was alone in the store a lot of the time. Therefore, she was "managing the store." And when she went shopping with her daughter for things to sell in the store, they were not "shopping" but "buying."

Give it a try. With a little help and an open mind, you too can develop a résumé that truly reflects you.

There's always a struggle, a striving for something bigger than yourself in all forms of art. And even if you don't achieve greatness—even if you fail, which we all must—everything you do in your work is somehow connected with your attitude toward life, your deepest secret feelings.

Rex Harrison,
as quoted in *The New York Times*

LAWRENCE A. DiCAPPA
1112 Vermont Lane
Downingtown, PA
(215) 555-1111

SUMMARY OF QUALIFICATIONS

<u>Extensive product knowledge</u> is coupled with <u>creative</u> ideas for product applications and a <u>solid history of sales success</u>. A proven ability to <u>develop sales potential in new market areas</u>. Strong analytical and planning skills, combined with the ability to coordinate the efforts of many to meet organizational goals. <u>Productive</u> and <u>efficient</u> work habits without supervision. Self-motivator and high energy.

PROFESSIONAL EXPERIENCE

A <u>solid background in sales and product experience</u>.
Additional <u>supervisory as well as training experience</u>.

EMPLOYMENT HISTORY

Telephone Sales Representative, AMP Special Industries   June, 1988-Present

- o <u>Achieved 140% growth</u> in assigned account responsibility: from $90,000 to $230,000 in the year 1989. Accounts were previously declining at 35% annually.

- o <u>Developed a complete marketing program where none previously existed</u>. Program now serves as a guide for new hires and future departmental growth.

- o <u>Set up and established new territory by</u>:
    - Devising a technique for <u>introducing the sales concept and then the product to customers.</u>
    - <u>Designing an introductory call script</u> which is now a standard for the department.
    - Developing a <u>strategy for attacking and penetrating a customer master list.</u>
    - Serving as product specialist and trainer for six new hires.
    - Developing <u>complete managerial outline</u> for continued growth and success of the department.

- o Finished in top three in both advanced and basic sales training classes.

DiCAPPA

EMPLOYMENT HISTORY, contd.

Office Manager, American Excelsior Company   1984 to 1988
     (approximately two years full-time while attending college)

    o   <u>Responsible for internal sales service</u>.

    o   <u>Purchased 70%</u> of company's <u>raw materials</u>.

    o   <u>Managed work flow</u> for an office of five personnel.

    o   <u>Coordinated the workload</u> of warehouse and trucking personnel in
             arranging shipments of customer orders via company-owned fleet and common
             carriers.

EDUCATION

B.S., Business Administration, Drexel University, Philadelphia, PA, 1988
    Major: Marketing, <u>4.0 Average in Field of Concentration.</u>

    <u>65% of total college expenses were earned through full-time and part-time employment.</u>

Homemaker's Résumé

1234 'XYZ' Street
City, State 11999
515-555-3456

Summary of Qualifications

The most important highlight of your experience is placed first. This is followed by your other experiences and skills. Perhaps you are an excellent administrator or organizer, work well with all kinds of people, or have some other special experience. The counselor will help determine the best way to express your strengths.

Professional Experience

Job Title or function you performed   dates or years
Company or organization name or project you worked on

- Here are listed some of the things you did there.
- **Think about what you *really* did, whether or not it was your job to do it**.
- It is *very* difficult to think about these things yourself. A career counselor is able to develop a résumé that reflects your experience. Your résumé will look like this one.

Another Job Title or function you performed   dates or years
Company or organization name or project you worked on

- A list of the things you did, **whether or not you were paid for them.**
- If the work you did was not for an organization, but was for family or friends, that's okay. We can make a résumé out of those experiences also.

PTA   1976 to present

- Maria thought her PTA experience was useless. But we expressed what she had done in a way that reflected her efforts. We can do the same for you. Do *not* compare your experiences to Maria's. Comparing yourself to someone else will prevent you from thinking about those things you truly did well, enjoyed doing, and are proud of.

- Instead, **think only about yourself**: What do *you* enjoy doing? What are you good at? What do you find yourself doing again and again? Do you find yourself "catering" parties for friends? Then, let's talk about it. Do you stage raffles for your church or synagogue? Let's talk about it. Have you held posts in an organization? What do others say about your work? What do *you* think about your work? Let's talk about it, and put it down on paper.

- I know you are proud of your husband and children. But instead of telling me about their accomplishments, tell me about yours. This may be difficult for you because you may be used to building them up instead of yourself. But we are not trying to get *them* a job. We're trying to get *you* a job, and so we have to talk about you and how good you are. Let's give it a try. Believe it or not, *everyone* comes out with a good résumé.

Coursework

We'll list here any courses you have taken if they are appropriate.

Maria Salerno

4756 Cashew Lane
Sweet Briar, Missouri 99000
999-555-3456

Summary of Qualifications

9 years' experience in office management and the fashion industry. 10 years as an officer or committee member for a not-for-profit organization. A thorough, conscientious and hard worker who meets deadlines and gets the job done. Works well with others including management, peers and the public.

Professional Experience

Salesperson/Store Manager (Part-time)   1-1/2 years
Propaganda Boutique, **(top-of-the-line women's clothing)**

- As Assistant Buyer, went to showrooms, selected clothing and accessories.
- Managed the store. Dealt with the public. Handled complaints.

Office Manager   3 years
Micro-Ohm Corporation
Office Manager for a 30-person company.

- Kept books, did the payroll, answered the phones.
- Regular contact with clients and employees. Worked closely with the President.

Bookkeeping Department
Lansing Knitwear (Also modeled clothing)   2 years
Chase Manhattan Bank   3 years

PTA   1976 to present

Over the course of 13 years, served as Vice President and on every Committee.
- Received **Certificate of Appreciation** for outstanding service and dedication.

- As **Vice President** (2 years),
  - Substituted for the President. Attended the Board meetings of all Committees.

- With members of the **International Committee,**
  - **Researched foreign countries**. Visited consulates. Recruited speakers.
  - **Held special events** to represent each country to the students. Served foreign foods, handed out flags, had dancers, or did whatever else was appropriate for that country.

- As a member of other committees,
  - **Recruited various speakers** to address the students.
  - These included a nutritionist, a computer expert, a Chinese cook, experts on drug and alcohol abuse, and so on. Also had **State senators and representatives** come in to address parents' concerns.

- As PTA Liaison, regularly meet with the Principal, Department Heads, and faculty members. Meetings are held to update the PTA, and to ask questions of the faculty.
- Serve as a delegate to other schools as a representative of the PTA.

Fluent in Italian; Familiar with Spanish.

VI. Résumé Checklist

1. Positioning:

- If I spend just **10 seconds** glancing at my résumé, what are the ideas/words that pop out? (specific job titles, my degrees, specific company names):

_____

- This is how I am "positioned" by my résumé. Is this how I want to be positioned for this target area? Or is this positioning a handicap for the area I am targeting?

2. Level:

- What **level** do I appear to be at? Is it easy for the reader to guess in 10 seconds what my level is? (For example, if I say I "install computer systems," I could be making anywhere from $15,000 a year to $200,000 a year.)

3. Summary Statement:

- If I have no summary statement, I am being positioned by the most recent job on my résumé. Is that how I want to be positioned?
- If I have a summary, does the very first line position me for the general kind of job I want next?
    - Is this followed by a statement that elaborates on the first statement?
    - Is this followed by statements that prove how good I am or differentiate me from my likely competitors?
    - Have I included a statement or two that give the reader an indication of my personality or my approach to my job?

4. Accomplishments:

- Within each job, did I merely list historically what I had done, or did I state my accomplishments with an eye to what would interest the reader in my target area?

- Are the accomplishments easy to read?
    - Bulleted rather than long paragraphs.
    - No extraneous words.
    - Action-oriented.
    - Measurable and specific.
    - Relevant. Would be of interest to the readers in my target area. Either the accomplishment is something they would want me to do for them, or it shows the breadth of my experience.

5. Overall Appearance:

- Is there plenty of white space? Or is the information squeezed so I can get it on one or two pages?
- Is it laid out nicely—so it can serve as my marketing brochure?

6. Miscellaneous:

- Length: Is the résumé as short as it can be while still being readable?
- Writing style: Can the reader understand the point I am trying to make in each statement?
- Clarity: Am I just hoping the reader will draw the right conclusion from what I've said? Or do I take the trouble to state things so clearly that there is no doubt that the reader will come away with the right message?
- Completeness: Is all important information included? Have all dates been accounted for?
- Typos: Is my résumé error-free?

This is the true joy in life, the being used for a purpose recognized by yourself as a mighty one, the being thoroughly worn out before you are thrown on the scrap heap; the being a force of nature instead of a feverish selfish little clod of ailments and grievances complaining that the world will not devote itself to making you happy.
George Bernard Shaw

I know you are asking today, "How long will it take?" I come to say to you this afternoon, however difficult the moment, however frustrating the hour, it will not be long, because truth pressed to earth will rise again.
How long? Not long, because no lie can live forever.
How long? Not long, because you still reap what you sow.
How long? Not long, because the arm of the moral universe is long but it bends towards justice.
How long? Not long, 'cause mine eyes have seen the glory of the coming of the Lord, trampling out the vinyards where the grapes of wrath are stored. He has loosed the fateful lightning of his terrible swift sword. His truth is marching on.
He has sounded forth the trumpets that shall never call retreat. He is lifting up the hearts of man before His judgment seat. Oh, be swift, my soul, to answer Him. Be jubilant, my feet. Our God is marching on.
Martin Luther King, Jr.

Dear sir, Be patient toward all that is unsolved in your heart and try to love the <u>questions themselves</u> like locked rooms and like books that are written in a very foreign tongue. Do not now seek the answers, which cannot be given you because you would not be able to live them. And the point is, to live everything. <u>Live</u> the questions now. Perhaps you will then gradually, without noticing it, live along some distant day into the answer. Perhaps you do carry within yourself the possibility of shaping and forming as a particularly happy and pure way of living; train yourself to it—but take whatever comes with trust, and if only it comes out of your own will, out of some need of your inmost being, take it upon yourself and hate nothing.
Ranier Maria Rilke, *Letters to a Young Poet*

The Five O'Clock Club:

- **Job-Search Strategy Groups**
- **Private Coaching**
- **Membership Information**

The Five O'Clock Club was founded by Kate Wendleton in 1978 to provide thoughtful career-development help for busy people of all levels. The programs and materials have helped thousands take control of their careers and find good jobs fast.

The original Five O'Clock Club was formed in Philadelphia in 1891. It was made up of the leaders of the day, who shared their experiences and fellowship "in a setting of sobriety and good humor."

Note: The following pages are taken from brochures and handouts of The Five O'Clock Club.

As a member of The Five O'Clock Club, you get:

❏ An attractive <u>membership card</u>, and a <u>Beginners' Kit</u> (valued at $15) containing information based on twelve years of research on who gets jobs . . . and why . . . that will enable you to improve your job-search techniques—immediately!

❏ A <u>free subscription</u> to *The Five O'Clock News*—ten issues filled with information on job search, résumé, cover letter, networking and interviewing techniques that have led to new careers for real people.

❏ Access to reasonably priced <u>weekly seminars</u> at local Affiliates, featuring individualized attention to your specific needs in small groups supervised by our senior counselors.

❏ Access to <u>one-on-one</u> counseling to help you answer specific questions, solve current job problems, prepare your résumé, or take an in-depth look at your career path.

❏ The opportunity to <u>exchange ideas</u> and experiences with other job searchers and career changers.

All that access, all that information, all that expertise for the annual membership fee of only $35.

How To Become a Member

Send your name, address, evening phone number, how you heard about us, and your check for $35 (payable to The Five O'Clock Club) to: The Five O'Clock Club, 1675 York Avenue-17D, NY, NY 10128. We will immediately mail you a Five O'Clock Club Membership Card, the Beginner's Kit, and information on our seminars.

Believe me, with self-examination and a lot of hard work with our counselors, you <u>can</u> find the job . . . you <u>can</u> have the career . . . you <u>can</u> live the life you always wanted!

Sincerely,
Kate Wendleton

The Five O'Clock Club Search Process

The Five O'Clock Club process, as outlined in Kate Wendleton's three books, *Through the Brick Wall*, the *Job Finder*, and the *Résumé Builder*, is a targeted, strategic approach to career development and job search. Five O'Clock Club members become proficient at skills which prove invaluable during their *entire working lives*.

We train our members to *manage their careers*, and always look ahead to their *next* job search. Research shows that an average worker spends only four years in a job—and will have 12 jobs, in as many as 5 career fields—during his or her working life.

Five O'Clock Club members find *better jobs, faster*. The average job search for a managerial position is now estimated at 8.1 months. The average Five O'Clock Club member who regularly attends weekly sessions finds a job by his or her tenth session. Even the discouraged, long-term job searcher can find immediate help.

The keystone to The Five O'Clock Club process is in teaching our members an understanding of the entire hiring process. A first interview is only a time for exchanging critical information. The real work starts after the interview. We teach our members *how to turn job interviews into offers*, and to negotiate the best possible employment package.

The Five O'Clock Club is *action-oriented*. **We'll help you decide what you should do this very next week to move your search along**. By their third session, our members have set definite job targets by industry or company size, position, and geographic location, and are out in the field, gathering information and making the contacts which will lead to interviews with hiring managers.

Our approach evolves with the changing job market. We're able to synthesize information from hundreds of Five O'Clock Club members, and come up with new approaches for our members. For example, we now discuss temporary placement for executives, how to handle voice mail, and how to network when doors are slamming shut all over town.

The Job-Search Strategy Group

The Five O'Clock Club meeting is a carefully planned *job-search strategy session*. We provide members with the tools and tricks necessary to get a good job fast—even in a tight market. Networking and emotional support are also included in the meeting.

The first part of the meeting is devoted to a forty-minute *main group presentation* on a particular aspect of job search; another part, to *small group strategy sessions* led by trained career consultants.

The *main group presentations* are given on a rotating schedule, so a job searcher can join The Five O'Clock Club at any time. Members are encouraged to attend ten sessions in a row, after which they are free to stay with the main group or switch to the *advanced discussion group*, if one is offered.

Your *small group strategy session* is your chance to get feedback and advice on your own search, listen to and learn from others, and build your business network. All groups are led by trained career consultants, who bring years of experience to your search. The small group is generally no more than eight to ten people, so everyone gets the chance to speak up.

The first fifteen minutes of every meeting are given over to *informal networking*; the fifteen minutes between the main lecture and the small group strategy sessions are set aside for members to report on new jobs. The meetings are information-packed and action-oriented, move rapidly, and give you the tools and incentive to keep your search going.

Private Coaching

Your local Affiliate can give you a list of career consultants available between group meetings for *private coaching*. Individual sessions help you answer specific questions, solve current job problems, prepare your résumé, or take an in-depth look at your career path. Please pay the consultant directly, as *private coaching is __not__ included in The Five O'Clock Club seminar or membership fee.*

For more information on becoming a member, please call:
212-289-1674, ext. 600

The
Five
O'Clock
Club®

The Five O'Clock Club means sobriety, refinement of thought and speech,
good breeding and good order. To this, much of its success is due.
The Five O'Clock Club is easy-going and unconventional.
A sense of propriety, rather than rules of order, governs its meetings.

J. Hampton Moore
History of The Five O'Clock Club
(written in the 1890's)

Just like the members of the original Five O'Clock Club, today's members want an ongoing relationship. George Vaillant, in his seminal work on successful people, found that "what makes or breaks our luck seems to be . . . our sustained relationships with other people." (George E. Vaillant, *Adaptation to Life*)

Five O'Clock Club members know that much of the program's benefit comes from simply showing up. Showing up will encourage you to do what you need to do when you are not here. And over the course of several weeks, certain things will become evident that are not evident now.

Five O'Clock Club members learn from each other: the group leader is not the only one with answers. The leader brings factual information to the meetings, and keeps the discussion in line. But the answers to some problems may lie within you, or with others in the group.

Five O'Clock Club members encourage each other. They listen, see similarities with their own situations, and learn from that. And they listen to see how they may help others. You may come across information or a contact that will help someone else in the group. Passing on that information is what we're all about.

If you are a new member here, listen to others to learn the process. And read the books so you will know the basics that others already know. When everyone understands the basics, this keeps the meetings on a high level, interesting, and helpful to everyone.

Five O'Clock Club members are in this together, but they know that ultimately they are each responsible for solving their own problems with God's help. Take the time to learn the process, and you will become better at analyzing your own situation, as well as the situations of others. You will be learning a method that will serve you the rest of your life, and in areas of your life apart from your career.

Five O'Clock Club members are kind to each other. They control their frustrations—because venting helps no one. Because many may be stressed, be kind and go the extra length to keep this place calm and happy. It is your respite from the world outside and a place for you to find comfort and FUN. Relax and enjoy yourself, learn what you can, and help where you can. And have a ball doing it.

There arises from the hearts of busy [people] a love of variety,
a yearning for relaxation of thought as well as of body,
and a craving for a generous and spontaneous fraternity.

J. Hampton Moore
History of The Five O'Clock Club

The original Five O'Clock Club was formed in Philadelphia in 1891. It was made up of the leaders of the day
who shared their experiences and fellowship "in a setting of sobriety and good humor."

Jargon and Terminology
Used at The Five O'Clock Club

Use The Five O'Clock Club terminology as a shorthand to express where you are in your job search. It will focus you and those in your group. The page numbers below refer to *Through the Brick Wall*, the basic text used at The Five O'Clock Club. Most people also use *Through the Brick Wall Job Finder*.

I.
Overview and Assessment

How many hours a week are you spending on your search?
Spend 35 hours on a full-time search; 15 hours on a part-time search.

What are your job targets?
Tell the group. A target includes industry or company size, position, and geographic area.

The group can help assess how good your targets are. Take a look at Measuring Your Job Targets (page 91).

How does your résumé position you?
The summary and body should make you look appropriate to your target.

What are your back-up targets?
Decide at the beginning of the search before the first campaign. Then you won't get stuck.

Have you done the Assessment?
If you have no specific targets, you cannot have a targeted search. Do the Assessment (Part II of *Through the Brick Wall*). You could see a counselor privately for two or three sessions to determine possible job targets.

II.
Getting Interviews

How large is your target area (e.g., thirty companies)? How many of them have you contacted?
Contact them all.

How can you get (more) leads?
You will not get a job through search firms, ads, networking or direct contact. Those are techniques for getting interviews—job leads. Use the right terminology, especially after a person gets a job. Do not say, "How did you get the job?" if you really want to know, "Where did you get the lead for that job?"

Do you have 6 to 10 things in the works?
You may want the group to help you land one job. After they help you with your strategy, they should ask, "How many other things do you have in the works?" If "none," the group can brainstorm how you can get more things going: through search firms, ads, networking, or direct contact. Then you are more likely to turn the job you want into an offer because you will seem more valuable. What's more, five will fall away through no fault of your own. Don't go after only one job.

How's your Two-Minute Pitch?
Practice a *tailored* Two-Minute Pitch. Tell the group the job title and industry of the hiring manager they should pretend they are for a role-playing exercise.

You will be surprised how good the group is at critiquing pitches. Do it a few weeks in a row until you have a smooth presentation.

Practice it again after you have been in search a while, or after you change targets. Make sure your pitch separates you from your competition.

You seem to be in Stage One (or Stage Two or Stage Three) of your search.

Know where you are in the process. If you are in Stage One—making initial contacts you will recontact later— make *lots* of contacts so at least 6 to 10 will move to Stage Two: the right people at the right levels in the right company. But at this stage, you may not be talking about actual jobs. You will get the best job offers in Stage Three—talking to 6 to 10 people on an ongoing basis about real jobs or the possibility of creating a job.

Are you seen as insider or outsider?

See Chapter 2 for becoming an insider. If people are saying, "I wish I had an opening for someone like you," you are doing well in meetings. If the industry is strong, then it's only a matter of time before you get a job.

III.
Turning Interviews into Offers

Do you want to go through the Brick Wall ?

Group members may have ideas for turning your job interview into an offer, only to get a lukewarm reception from you. If you do not want the job, perhaps you want an offer, if only for practice. If you are not willing to go for it, the group's suggestions will not work.

Who are your likely competitors and how can you "kill them off"?

"Kill the competition" does not mean dirty tricks, but reminds you that you have competitors. You will not get a job simply because "they liked me." The issues are deeper. Ask the interviewer: "Where are you in the hiring process? What kind of person would be your ideal candidate?"

What are your next steps?

The "next step" means: what are *you* planning to do if the hiring manager doesn't call by a certain date, or what are you planning to do to assure that the hiring manager *does* call you? (See *Through the Brick Wall*, Chapter 26, Planning Your Follow-Up.)

Can you prove you can do the job?

Most job hunters take the "Trust me—I can handle the job" approach. (See *Through the Brick Wall*, Chapter 25, Consider Your Competition.)

Which job positions you best for the long run? Which job is the best fit?

Don't decide only on the basis of salary. Since the average person has been in his or her job only four years, you will most likely have another job after this. See which job looks best on your résumé, and makes you a stronger candidate next time.

In addition, find a fit for your personality. If you don't "fit," it is unlikely you will do well there. The group can give feedback on which job is best for you.

The
Five
O'Clock
Club®

Application for Membership

Application
for membership in
The Five O'Clock Club®

"For those who care about their careers"

☐ Yes! I want access to the most effective methods for finding jobs, as well as for developing and managing my career.

I enclose my check for $35.00 (U.S. dollars), made payable to The Five O'Clock Club, for which I will receive a Beginner's Kit (valued at $15.00), a membership card, a 1-year subscription to The Five O'Clock News, access to a network of career counselors and to seminars at Affiliates of The Five O'Clock Club throughout the U.S. and Canada.

PLEASE CLEARLY PRINT ALL INFORMATION:

Name_____

Address_____

City_____State_____Zip_____

Country_____

Home Phone (_____)_____

Work Phone (_____)_____

Today's Date:_____

Referred by:_____

The following information is for statistical purposes only.
Thanks for your help.

Age: ☐ under 20   ☐ 20-29   ☐ 30-39   ☐ 40-49   ☐ 50+

Sex: ☐ Male   ☐ Female

Salary range:

☐ under $30,000   ☐ $30 - $49,999   ☐ $50 - $79,999

☐ $80 - $99,999   ☐ $100 - $199,999   ☐ $200 - $500,000

Current or most recent position/title:

_____

Note: Fees may change without prior notice.

Page numbers in *italics* denote notable people and works mentioned or quoted.
Page numbers in **boldface** denote the main discussion of that topic.

Index

About the Author

Kate Wendleton is a nationally recognized authority on career development. She has been a career coach since 1978, when she founded and developed The Five O'Clock Club® methodology to help job hunters and career changers of all levels in job-search-strategy groups. This methodology is now used by Affiliates of The Five O'Clock Club, which meet weekly from Harlem to Oregon, Toronto to Texas, from The Yale Club to local community colleges.

Kate also founded Workforce America™, a not-for-profit Affiliate of The Five O'Clock Club serving adults in Harlem who are not yet in the professional or managerial ranks. Workforce America helps each person move into better-paying, higher-level positions as each improves in educational level and work experience.

Kate founded, and directed for seven years, The Career Center at The New School for Social Research in New York. She also counsels executives for major corporations, such as Citibank. A former CFO of two small companies, she has twenty years of business-management experience in both manufacturing and service businesses.

Kate attended Chestnut Hill College in Philadelphia and received her MBA from Drexel University. She is a popular speaker with groups that include The Wharton Business School Club, the Yale Club, The Columbia Business School Club, and Workforce America in Harlem.

While living in Philadelphia, Kate did long-term volunteer work for The Philadelphia Museum of Art, The Walnut Street Theatre Art Gallery, United Way, and the YMCA. Kate currently lives in Manhattan.

Kate Wendleton is also the author of *Through the Brick Wall: How to Job-Hunt in a Tight Market*, the *What Color Is Your Parachute?* of the nineties and the *Through the Brick Wall Job Finder*.